The Book of
COLNEY HEATH
ST ALBANS

Out of the Wilderness

BRYAN LILLEY

With a Foreword by the Rt Revd and Rt Hon.
Lord Runcie of Cuddesdon

HALSGROVE

First published in Great Britain in 2002

Frontispiece photograph: *The lively scene as Morris dancers entertain outside the Crooked Billet.*

British Library Cataloguing-in-Publication Data
A CIP record for this title is available from the British Library

ISBN 1 84114 159 3

HALSGROVE
PUBLISHING, MEDIA AND DISTRIBUTION

Halsgrove House
Lower Moor Way
Tiverton, Devon EX16 6SS
Tel: 01884 243242
Fax: 01884 243325
email: sales@halsgrove.com
website: www.halsgrove.com

Printed and bound by
Bookcraft Ltd, Midsomer Norton

Every care has been taken to ensure the accuracy of the information contained in this book. The author recognises, however, that errors and omissions will inevitably be found, and he regrets any inadvertent mistakes.

Contents

DEDICATION

For Richard, Ruth and Alison,
who grew up in Colney Heath and
were baptised at St Mark's Church.

The Author

While resident in Colney Heath, Bryan Lilley served on the Parochial Church Council, Hatfield Deanery Synod and St Albans Diocesan Synod. For seven years – one as Chairman – he was an elected member of Colney Heath Parish Council.

He was the first public relations officer appointed by Welwyn Hatfield District Council. In 1986 an appointment in county government brought him to Lincolnshire as head of public relations for the County Council. In 1995 he was invited to serve on Lincoln Diocesan Advisory Committee for the Care of Churches. At this time his wider responsibility was for pastorally redundant churches in the northeast. Vested in The Churches Conservation Trust, established by Parliament and the General Synod, these churches – no longer in parochial use – are considered to be worthy of safeguarding because of their special significance to the nation.

In March 1999 Bryan Lilley was appointed Secretary to Lincoln DAC. He manages the administration of faculty jurisdiction in the largest territorial diocese in England, covering some 2673 square miles from the Humber to The Wash. It possesses much of the finest ecclesiastical architecture in Britain and some 650 churches, of which 65 per cent are Grade I or Grade II* listed buildings.

Since the span of years allotted to us is short, let us leave something behind to show that we have lived.

– Sir Francis Dashwood

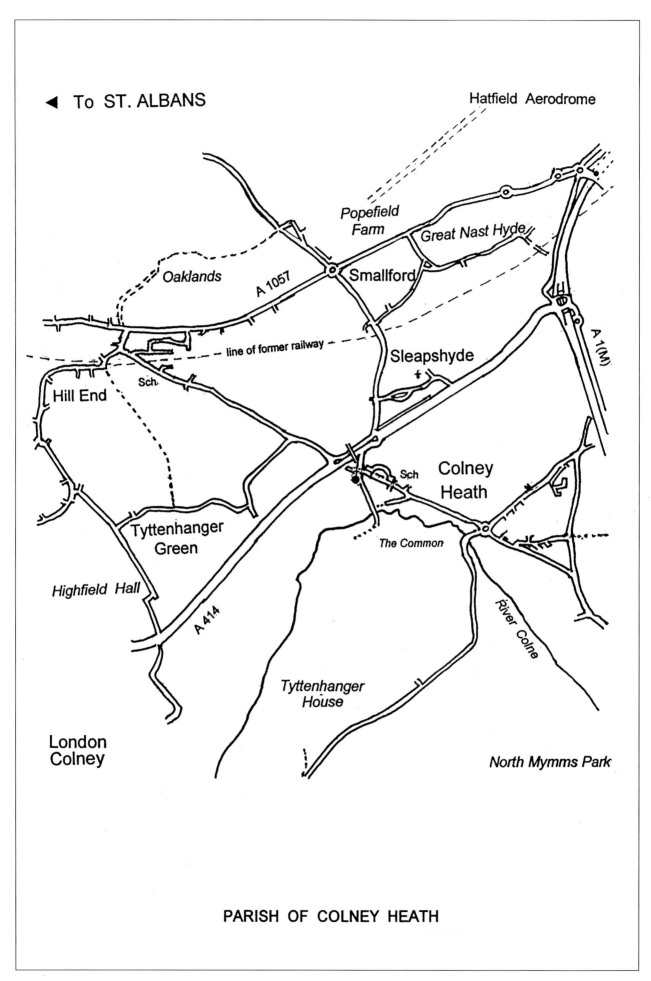

◄ To ST. ALBANS

Hatfield Aerodrome

Popefield Farm

Great Nast Hyde

Oaklands

A 1057

Smallford

line of former railway

Sleapshyde

A 1(M)

Sch.

Hill End

Sch

Colney Heath

Tyttenhanger Green

The Common

Highfield Hall

A 414

River Colne

Tyttenhanger House

London Colney

North Mymms Park

PARISH OF COLNEY HEATH

Foreword

I keep a little corner of my home library for parish histories. This will be a delightful addition. Anyone who is interested in our part of Hertfordshire will be fascinated by the tale so clearly, accurately and elegantly told; but, as with all the best books of this sort, it is a prism through which you see the changing customs of a country and a people. It is the story of the creation of a new parish centred on a charming little church and those who have been charged with its care and the 'cure of souls' – that old traditional phrase for the spiritual welfare of all the people.

The account of the consecration throws a spotlight on church development in the middle of a century of growth for the Church of England. One of the great organisers of that growth was Charles Blomfield, the Bishop of London. We think of him as one who created the present central administration of our Church; he worked with Sir Robert Peel and the young Mr Gladstone. The fair distribution of wealth would produce churches and vicarages where there were none before.

It was an exciting day in December 1845 when this national figure came to Colney Heath for the consecration. It was the most rural outpost of his diocese and he was shortly to shed Hertfordshire, which had a strange ecclesiastical history, before it was taken into the Diocese of St Albans in 1877. It was muddy and we have a picture of the gentry arriving in their carriages. Charles Blomfield stayed the night before with his brother in Stevenage and the following night in the country house, Oaklands, east of St Albans. Significantly, he preached on the text 'The poor shall have the Gospel preached to them'.

The evangelical movement that brought the Gospel to many more of the ordinary folk of our land, as well as led so many reforming movements under Wilberforce and Shaftesbury, is seen here creating a little church and parish out of a wilderness. The new church was paid for by the prosperous, but when the time came, the money and voluntary labour from the village surprised the nobs of St Peter's in St Albans. The building is really a memorial to the energy and missionary spirit of Horatio Nelson Dudding, vicar of St Peter's and founder of the church in Colney Heath.

Nothing is clearer from this story than the sturdy independence and character of St Mark's. That is the message that seems to come quietly through the procession of local characters and vicars. It is not a place dependent upon the big house or the lord of the manor. It is not a church that has to be propped up by the diocese. It works out its own salvation, for it is confident in Paul's words that 'Christ works within us'.

Not surprisingly there have been incumbents who have given their all to this parish. The strength of the church in Colney Heath must depend a lot upon this fact. It may not have many famous names and has not produced bishops but it is none the worse for that. Indeed, its strength lies in the way in which new circumstances raise new opportunities for the spread of the Gospel and the building up of God's people. When I was Bishop there was the marvellously faithful ministry of Joe Butland. In his days the church confronted the growing number of young people with vigour, developing the Sunday school, then Pathfinders and groups for young marrieds.

The parish was split by the creation of the hazardous North Orbital Road. Yet, characteristically, Joe Butland led the campaign to make crossing safer and to the people of St Mark's a debt is owed for maintaining the character of the community when it would have been very easy for it to fall into a dormitory area on the edge of St Albans.

So today there is a clear continuation of thriving church life – angled towards nourishing the young people in a vibrant faith but never forgetting the church's responsibility to care for the whole people of God. This book throws a flood of light on the consistency and energy, which out of a deprived rural area gave rise to a strong semi-urban parish – in the same way, the brook that runs through the village, gradually becomes the Colne, flows on through Watford and eventually into the mainstream of the Thames. There is no need to despair about the Church of England or to be dismayed about its future when you read of the resilience and character of the parish of Colney Heath.

The Right Reverend and Right Hon. Lord Runcie of Cuddesdon

Robert Alexander Kennedy Runcie MC, former principal of Cuddesdon Theological College, Oxford, was appointed Bishop of St Albans in 1970. In 1980 he was translated as Archbishop of Canterbury. Lord Runcie retired in 1991 and died on 11 July 2000 at his home in St Albans.

Acknowledgements

In graciously contributing the Foreword to this book, the Right Revd Lord Runcie accorded it a splendid beginning. Social and political history featured high among Lord Runcie's many interests, yet here his generosity is recalled encouraging what is, unquestionably, a parochial story. During his ten years as diocesan bishop in St Albans he met with the challenges and opportunities facing Colney Heath. Memorably from St Mark's pulpit, in the archiepiscopate years and in retirement, as well as in the commendation of this book, we are reminded of his personal faith and sound counsel about the place of the Church in society. We have good cause to remember, with gratitude and affection, Lord Runcie's interest in the parish of Colney Heath on the fringe of his beloved St Albans.

There has long been a desire to record Colney Heath's modern social history. Only limited archival material was available at the celebration of the one hundred and twenty-fifth anniversary of the ecclesiastical parish – then the parallel civil parish had been established for just 23 years. Support for a published history came from Colney Heath and District Local History Society and two past incumbents, the Revd W.E. Butland (vicar between 1958 and 1980) and his successor, the Revd D.R. Veness (vicar from 1980 to 1998). The latter granted access to a store of village and parochial records rediscovered in 1988.

I must thank Mr Paul Mason, who had begun cataloguing parish records. Mr Tony Bralant made plain the complexities of the church organ and Mr Brian Anderson has given unstintingly of his time and good advice as well as contributing photographs.

The village History Society has skillfully interpreted much archive material for wider public enjoyment. This perspective, witnessing across 150 years a community transformed from the anonymity of wilderness into a modern civil and ecclesiastical parish, was encouraged by two exceptionally gifted and greatly missed personalities: Malcolm Robertson Tomkins, the history society's first chairman, and H. Dudley Wood, another founder member, who served as the versatile and learned clerk to the Parish Council. Their knowledge of Colney Heath was unsurpassed.

In piam memoriam R.A.K.R., M.R.T., H.D.W.

Bryan Lilley
Verulam,
Wellingore,
Lincolnshire
St Faith's Day, 6 October 2001

Introduction

The celebration of 150 years in the life of a community affords opportunity to pause and reflect. When glancing at beginnings, considering the present and looking to the future, there can be no better reflection than that mirrored in the creation of a new English parish. It is a window touching the life of everyone. At Colney Heath we see the impoverishment of the wilderness years, petitioning for a church, the advent of the railway, demands for better education, the agonies wrought by two world wars and, in a rich tapestry throughout, the part played by colourful local personalities.

That old maxim, 'Past is Prologue', owes much to the idea that people are conditioned, to a degree at least, by major events touching their lives. Examining a particular period of history, as reflected in Colney Heath's church-less rural community's entry into England's parochial system, provides not only a chronological commentary on village life but some startling glimpses, too, of the conditions facing early settlers and those following them.

Enhancing a community with parish status is certain to reveal some intriguing insights; it cannot be otherwise, whether an inherited church building is perceived now as ancient or modern, contemporarily primitive or architecturally intricate. While fulfilling its dedicated purpose, the church becomes also a repository of history. Yet the researcher knows that the facts presented by the archives together with the 'sermon of the stones' can never capture the whole story.

The community holds a remarkable record in achieving parish status; there are surprises down through the years. The little church in Colney Heath – the epitome of Emerson's hamlet church – was contemplated in difficult social times, early in the reign of Queen Victoria. Emerging in a period of significant religious revival in Britain, it met an urgent need for a local presence of the Established Church in a largely neglected rural area. Pleaded for in 1842, building work started in 1843. Fashioned in the Traditional Norman style, the village church opened for worship in June 1845 and the consecration by the Bishop of London took place at the very end of that year.

Over a century and a half later, St Mark's has earned a place more durable than Emerson's 'part of the sky' imagery concedes. The modest little building and its mission have become integrated into community life. The continuing ministry began even before occupancy of the first grand parsonage house. Here is much more than an ecclesiological study, for in the silence of the church's built stones as well as in its sounds – both sacred and secular – we are offered a lesson in humility and an apposite benchmark at the dawn of a new millennium.

Sometimes people aspire to what they become not because of history's hand but in spite of it. Lives can be enriched by the study of the past, through which we take reference for our own place. It is right that we pause to reflect upon the inheritance received from our forebears and to derive knowledge from history about our tenancy on earth.

Bryan Lilley

Chapter One

Firstcomers & A Founder

'THE WILDERNESS & THE SOLITARY PLACE...'

In the summer of 1979 a well-preserved George II penny-piece surfaced on the gravel at Park Corner, Colney Heath. A 'treasure' for two children returning home from rides on the miniature railway at the water works, the discovery led to some vying for ownership as well as an instant history lesson. Perhaps it was a lesson, too, for the most sceptical of the theory that Colney Heath, of all places, might lay claim to an interesting, if not noteworthy, past.

The sceptics had a point. Not much had happened before the place became a small settlement named after its wild terrain – infested with rabbits – stretching either side of an often flooded river-bank. For years this inhospitable landscape, four miles east of St Albans, was renowned only as the meeting point of the boundaries of four ancient parishes, far from the heart of their communities. Dominated by the scrub, this uninhabited heart of a rambling domain augured danger for the unwary traveller. For generations the daunting territory had remained a solitary and changeless place. That the heath was used by travellers to Verulamium is certain: a Roman track across it has been traced, along with artefacts and coin collections of the times.

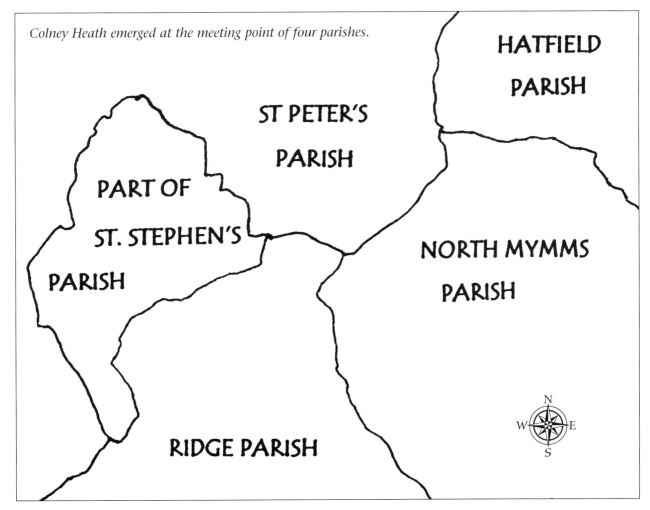

Colney Heath emerged at the meeting point of four parishes.

HATFIELD PARISH

ST PETER'S PARISH

PART OF ST. STEPHEN'S PARISH

NORTH MYMMS PARISH

RIDGE PARISH

Happy summer trips are enjoyed by old and young alike on Colney Heath's own miniature railway.

The common as a wilderness and solitary place.

The river comes close to High Street homes. Photo: Weston Marchant.

Arable farming remains a principal activity in Colney Heath parish.

Possibly the children's eighteenth-century penny already lay buried in 1777 when the line of Colney Heath's present High Street – then known as Old Banke – appeared on a map denoting just a few buildings. Crammed closely together on the favoured higher ground above the river – a natural place for the sparse population to gather – were the people's primitive wooden-clad dwellings. About ten years earlier, a Drury map had confirmed the shrinking heathland due to annexing for timber-built shelters. The original heath was a vast area, but by 1331 a survey of the Manor of Tyttenhanger had shown it depleted to 200 acres, largely within Ridge parish, south of the river. At that time the heath was given over to pasture with common grazing rights. The present public heathland, now secured by the Parish Council and registered as a common, covers about 60 acres.

Around the map-making time of 1766, a first brief comment appears about the lack of influence held at Colney Heath by the Church. The Tyttenhanger park-keeper testified: 'The minister of St Peter's (St Albans) never used to go a-processing with his parish farther than the highway.' This also suggests that the estate laid claim to land northward, beyond the river and up to the road.

Farmsteads were the first taming influence on Colney Heath's wilderness. They represented a modest livelihood and stability for the poor population and generated the most soundly constructed buildings to be seen. Some holdings stood in strange detachment, such as Paxton's farmhouse, which, dating from the end of the seventeenth century, did not grace Coursers Road – originally Bell Lane – until the link to London Colney, constructed in 1805, swept by close to the house. Soundly built, too, and a considerable cut above the profusion of alehouses springing up – one for every ten cottages in the early days of the village – were the hostelries, notably the Cock and the Queen's Head. Both establishments pre-date the founding of the church at Colney Heath by 100 years.

The main thoroughfare from the earliest times was a twisting, dusty, unmetalled lane. It had changed little by the time the young Princess Victoria came to the throne in 1837. This 'highway' was entirely within St Peter's parish and skirted the equally far-flung outposts of the St Albans parish of St Stephen and that of Ridge. It was used by carts trundling between North Mymms and St Albans.

There were occasional visitations by the clergy of St Peter's sprawling parish. They reached Colney Heath conspicuously by horse-drawn carriage. The preachers' concerns for this unchurched backwater led, in 1814, to the opening of a modest schoolroom in the High Street. Sited where Scholars Court stands today, the primitive building provided scripture classes for children and adults on Sundays and elementary education for weekday pupils. It was a bold attempt to bring the Christian message and basic learning to a deprived people. Still remaining on the south side of the High Street is the red-brick house built for the schoolmaster at about the time the schoolroom took on charitable status as a pioneering church day school. Tuition was provided also for 'labouring class' adults in the evenings. Those not reached by itinerant clergy rarely saw inside a church or attended anywhere for worship. Marriages, funerals and baptisms, however, did mean getting to St Peter's somehow, usually on foot. The very few from the village outskirts attending

The High Street looking east around 1900. 'Beta', the two bothy cottages on the left, are thatched. Beyond, the Crooked Billet may just be seen across the road from the original school buildings.

The same view 75 years on.

ancient parish churches in the neighbourhood were most likely to be 'carriage folk'.

Some Colney Heath people attended worship where it was possible to walk to a distant church. This was despite foregoing rights to the occasional offices because they had strayed from St Peter's parish. Such journeys presented problems. While Ridge parish boundary swept right up to Park Corner, its little church of St Margaret, four and a half miles away, could not be reached easily even after the making of Coursers Road. However, the new road did improve access to London Colney and its new church of St Peter, built in 1825.

Strictly by invitation was the rare opportunity to attend service at the nearest place of worship. This was south of the common across the fields at Tyttenhanger, one of the most graceful houses to survive from the rebuilding era of the mid-seventeenth century. It became the mainland seat of the Alexander family, awarded an Irish peerage in 1880 as Earls of Caledon. Services were held in the second-floor chapel on the north side of the house. The tiny room, panelled in Elizabethan linenfold, had the comfort of an open fireplace; above this a mural panel showing the Ten Commandments. Set aside with altar and a two-decker pulpit fitted with an hourglass for timing sermons, the chapel was consecrated by the Bishop of Exeter during Cromwell's Commonwealth.

When the house and contents were sold by James, the sixth earl, in June 1972, the legal elements of consecration remained in the chapel but some fine furniture and fittings came under the hammer of Ralph Pay & Ransom, the West End auctioneers handling the sale. One item, the ivory and wooden crucifix mounted behind the pulpit – together with four unimportant pictures – fetched just £75; it was later discovered that the pulpit cross, the work of an Italian sculptor, was identified as being 'beyond price'. Both Cardinal Wolsey and Henry VIII were staying guests at the pre-1654 Tyttenhanger. A month before the present property was sold the last royal visitor was Queen Elizabeth the Queen Mother, who in May 1972 was entertained by the earl and countess at a swansong tea party.

Tyttenhanger House

*Tyttenhanger House in the days
of formal gardens in 1905.*
Photo: Country Life.

Right: *The chapel at Tyttenhanger with a two-decker
pulpit complete with hourglass.* Photo: Country Life.

*The formal
gardens have
gone, as have
the two French
doors (left).*

Relatively near at Hatfield, St Etheldreda's was to the north-east, while eastward St Mary's ancient church in North Mymms Park made a pleasant walk in summer months. The difficulties confronting Colney Heath folk travelling very far were real. Even getting to St Albans was not straightforward: the old Hatfield Road was not reconstructed until 1824.

Effectively those in Colney Heath's 'wilderness' had remained in much the same state for years, right up to the early-nineteenth century. The population subsisted but had little prospect, or so it seemed, of ever achieving more than hamlet status. Nobody had visions of being part of a flourishing village community. The suggestion that one day there would be a Victorian parish church boasting an outer stone stairway styled after the Norman one at The King's School, Canterbury, would have been beyond the people's wildest dream.

All quiet in less busy days where Coursers Road, High Street, Roestock Lane and Tollgate Road meet.

LEGACY OF NEGLECT

Only the staunch few from Colney Heath habitually presented themselves at their parish church in St Albans at Easter. Turnout was better for baptisms, marriages and to bury the dead. Indeed, funerals were by far the most compelling reason to seek ministration at St Peter's and thereby secure a place in the commodious churchyard.

Keeping the sexton busy was a reflection of the one-sided flow of penitents from Colney Heath in the first four decades of the nineteenth century. Hygiene, as much as desire for the final Christian ritual, dictated the unseemly haste of funeral processions leaving the village for St Albans. These foot processions were a familiar scene at a time known, not for longevity but, rather, high infant mortality. Generally, lifespans of the labouring classes, who numbered around 450 in the village, were fairly short.

For lightness on their final journey, bodies, swathed in shrouds, were carried in wicker coffins by teams of up to six bearers. Those who 'went carrying' wore black mourning as a rule, and sometimes bands of white, and the size of the burden indicated an infant or child burial. Although relieved in their carrying shifts across the fields, bearers were careful to choose the shortest route from Colney Heath to St Albans. They used a network of footpaths and bridleways, still in existence, which were known as the Corpse Way.

The combination of distance from St Albans and the difficulty in attending Divine Service led some in Colney Heath to set up a string of ad-hoc religious meetings in their homes. These meetings were of some concern to the Church authorities of the day. Outwardly, however, there was little evidence of much influence being exercised by the then Established and United Church of England and Ireland.

Around the beginning of the nineteenth century, a tenant of Colney Heath landlady, Sarah

*St Peter's Church, St Albans,
which before 1845 was
the parish church for
Colney Heath.*

The first house in Colney Heath from Sleapshyde – known as 'Alpha' – was renamed 'Moonrakers' in honour of the winner of the 1832 St Albans steeple-chase. The house was pulled down in 1967 to make way for new development.

*The apple tree survives in front of the modern 'Moonrakers';
next door is the much altered 'Beta', also renamed.*

Pursetts, is recorded as having set up a registered place of worship for the benefit of Protestant dissenters. By 1804, John Brooks' barn was being used as a meeting-place for other dissenters. With thoughts of putting a brake on the way things were going, the Church authorities in St Albans began seriously to consider what should be done. Another ten years passed before the parish school-room was built in the centre of the south side of the High Street. The building was entirely funded from public donations. The foundation stone has the inscription:

SUNDAY SCHOOL HOUSE
belonging to St Peter's Parish
Built by voluntary subscription, 1814

It was preserved when the old schoolroom was demolished in 1969. As an artefact of the history of education in the village, the stone may be seen in Colney Heath's modern primary school where it is set into the wall of the entrance lobby. Hertfordshire County Council's education authority and, earlier, the School Board, had used the old parish buildings as classrooms for about 100 of their 155 years' existence.

Despite the purpose of the 1814 simple brick and rendered building, designed to bring Christian instruction and education to Colney Heath's people, Protestant dissenters were congregating in greater numbers. By January 1827 a large assembly was meeting at the now demolished Butterwick Farm, off Sleapshyde Lane. This was the home of John Lampkin, described as a 'High Calvinist'. That summer Lampkin was also attending the meetings of Baptists and Independents, who gathered at the High Street home of John Willson. He lived in a pleasant eighteenth-century white rendered house in the middle of the main street on the north side, directly opposite Park Lane. As the first property in the village, coming in from Sleapshyde, the house took naturally to the name, Alpha. Next door, Beta was a pair of timber-framed diminutive thatched bothy cottages dating from around 1700. Next came a pretty rendered cottage, then the Crooked Billet, which apart from a cluster of wooden houses to its east, brought to an end this 'built up' part of the High Street as suddenly as it had begun.

One occupier of the first house found himself the winner of the 'St Albans Grand Steeple Chase' which used to finish on the common at a point opposite the house. On 8 March 1832 the horse, Moonraker, finished the course of nearly four and a half miles in a record time of just over 15 minutes. In honour of the achievement the owner renamed his house after the horse. The name survived the between-the-wars numbering which

made the property 96 High Street. The old house was pulled down in 1967 to make way for new development. Its history, however, is called to mind in the nameplate retained on the modern house built on the site for the writer whose family home it was for 26 years.

By 1835 the Wesleyan Methodists had established a group of 19 members in the district. Six years on they had built the little chapel at Sleapshyde. If this development caused any worries in the Archdeaconry of St Albans, there were no problems among local people who welcomed the opening of the chapel. On leaving Colney Heath after 20 years, the Revd Laurence Bomford (vicar between 1898 and 1918) paid tribute to the Wesleyans' 'strenuous efforts to supply ministrations to the people'.

Laurence Bomford chronicled earlier days of lawlessness at Colney Heath. There was great appeal for prizefighting on the common, staged by organisations known as the Gentlemen of St Albans and the Gentlemen of Barnet. This was given added impetus because the river bank marked the division between the metropolitan and county police districts, making it easy for illegal fighters to operate on either side of the boundary and temporarily evade the law. Dubious field sports were rife and poaching was another favourite pastime.

As late as 1800 highwaymen and footpads were making the common a place to be avoided. Heavy betting on cock fights and on prize-fighting was normal with vast assemblies recorded in 1831. Card-sharpers thought it worth coming out from London to rook their opponents and they were still arriving in great numbers into the 1840s.

Despite the Gaming Act of 1831, Colney Heath continued to attract various unlawful activities. The place had become a brash, noisy haven for wrongdoers. Those looking for better things suggested that Colney Heath's remoteness, increasing lawlessness and growth of dissenters spelled extreme urgency for action. By action they meant it was time for this neglected backwater to have its own place of worship, ordered by the rites and ceremonies of the Church of England.

In the first tentative approaches made to the Church hierarchy, criminality was set aside in the evidence given. Concentration was made, instead, on the distance of Colney Heath from any Established Church building. If a new church was to be built in the centre of the village, it was argued that 300 people who lived more than two miles away from an Anglican church would find themselves within one mile of their own parish church. The figures and the prospect were undeniably attractive.

The 'St Albans Grand Steeple Chase' of 1832 is won by Moonraker, here crossing the winning line at Colney Heath just half a neck ahead of Grimaldi.

The Colne used to divide the metropolitan and county police areas, giving opportunity for the law to be evaded

CREATING A NEW PARISH - THE LINCOLNSHIRE CONNECTION

Events leading to Colney Heath being given parish status and having its own church were dramatic. A leader was needed; somebody who could set the people on a better path and motivate them out of poverty of spirit: it was easier said than done. There was no better allegory for the situation than the Old Testament account of the Jordan waters being cut off to allow the people of Israel to pass from the desert to the promised land.

Who was to be the rescuing Joshua of the middle of the nineteenth century? Who would set place in Colney Heath not 12 great stones marking a great deliverance, but the House of God? Its building would signal that, indeed, the people had been led from their wilderness. Answers were not readily to hand. However, nobody doubted that the right person, a true leader, would be raised up.

If events at this time were to prove remarkable, so was the reputa- tion of the person destined to steer them. The enormous task was to fall on the shoulders of a young man who was to influence very greatly the social and religious issues in St Albans for more than half a century. He was to exercise the most profound impact upon Colney Heath.

The leader-elect's antecedents can be traced through one family settled on the remote north- western outpost of Lincolnshire. There, on a bleak, commanding hilltop stands Alkborough, where stone-built cottages cluster round the partly Anglo-Saxon church. One Robert Dudding, born of yeoman stock in 1480, found himself following in a family tradition in this, the most northern parish of the Province of Canterbury.

In 1538 Dudding was appointed church- warden at the parish church which had been given to Spalding Priory in 1052; he had charge of records tracing incumbents back to the year 1220. To this day the church remains pervaded by an aura of antiquity, mystery and holiness. Churchwarden Dudding served Alkborough well. From the top of St John the Baptist's tower he could gaze westward across a dramatic landscape of rivers and flat lands to the confluence of the Ouse and Trent as they become the great Humber

river. To the east lay Spurn Point and, northward, York Minster. There were majestic, sweeping views, to the southern horizon, in the direction of the great triple towers of the cathedral at Lincoln.

At this time the enormous diocese of Lincoln stretched from the Humber's south bank to Oxfordshire at Dorchester-on-Thames. One of the bishop's palaces was at Buckden – around the halfway point – a fair compromise bearing in mind most of the bishop's travelling would have been on horseback. The huge See included the Archdeaconry of St Albans, embracing the modest town renowned for harbouring Britain's Christian pro-martyr, whose sacrifice had given the place its name.

If Robert Dudding ever gave St Albans a moment's thought from his vantage point beneath the skyscapes of Lindsey's rolling arable acres, he had little cause to think that, one day, a direct descen- dant would become a key figure in that distant place, 180 miles south. That member of the Dudding family was to prove to be a most illus- trious citizen of St Albans and a remarkable occupant at St Peter's Vicarage from where he exercised a ministry for over 50 years. Ten generations on, scripture's words of deliverance were to weigh heavily on the Dudding to be appointed incumbent of St Peter's. He was the Revd Horatio Nelson Dudding; he was driven by a great personal concern for the people of Colney Heath. Coming from rural Suffolk, he hit St Albans like a whirlwind, immediately setting in motion a plan to secure a church for the wilderness area of his prosperous town-centre parish. This caring, learned, scholar-priest had begun an effective ministry to the people; he was just 34 years old.

Inset: *The Dudding family can be traced back to roots in 1480 in the parish of St John the Baptist, in Alkborough, Lincolnshire.*

THE FOUNDER

The Revd Horatio Nelson Dudding, Vicar of St Peter's, St Albans 1842–1895

Horatio was a popular name in the early years of the nineteenth century following the Battle of Trafalgar in 1805. In the case of the Dudding family it was bestowed for more than whimsical reasons upon the second son of Edward Barr Dudding and his wife, Mary, of the parish of St Peter, Normanby-by-Spital, 12 miles north of Lincoln. The couple had married in 1797.

Before the marriage, Mary (née Nelson), lived in the north of Lincolnshire at Great Limber, a village on the 28,000-acre Brocklesby estate of the Pelhams (earls of Yarborough). Her family's most illustrious son, Horatio Nelson, was yet to rise in the Royal Navy to become Admiral of the Fleet and end up with a peerage as the first Earl Nelson of Merton and The Nile.

It was not only patriotic but most appropriate that Edward and Mary's son, born on 21 September 1808 – three years after Trafalgar – should be baptised Horatio. At the same time, the opportunity was taken to add the famous seafarer's surname to the Dudding family name, and there it has remained. Young Horatio's father left rural Lincolnshire and came to London where he became successful in a pioneer business: printing designs on furnishing fabrics. Edward Dudding had two houses, one in London near the business and the other in St Albans. He died in London in 1830 and is buried in St Peter's churchyard, St Albans.

Horatio proved to be a bright pupil at school. At Oxford he distinguished himself as a classical scholar, graduating with first-class honours – *Literae Humaniores*. He was awarded a master's degree in 1831 and went on to become a don and Fellow of Exeter College. Five years later, following theological studies, he was ordained deacon, remaining in Oxford to serve his title at St Ebbe's where he stayed for just over a year.

The year 1837 was eventful. Victoria came to the throne, Nelson Dudding married Margaret Haydon and, at the end of the year, he gave up lecturing at Oxford for a move to Suffolk. He was appointed to the rectory at Stonham Parva, near Stowmarket. His institution in the fourteenth-century church of St Mary the Virgin was by the Bishop of Norwich, whose diocese in those days included Suffolk.

Not yet 30, the rector quickly earned himself a reputation as a powerful, eloquent preacher. His extempore style pleased packed congregations and he was never seen reading from notes when in the pulpit. Nelson Dudding left the rural idyll after more than four years. He moved to St Albans in March 1842 and was presented for the living at St Peter's on 30 April. Faced with a huge parish of around 3,720 souls out of St Albans' 7,000 population, the newly appointed pious and evangelical vicar was immediately consumed in high activity. He was soon to find himself the energetic founder of the new church and parish at Colney Heath, having identified its poor population as 'a Lazarus living at our gate'.

The new vicar had a practical bent as well as a colourful turn of phrase. These he put to use together as he canvassed the town-dwelling parishioners and the gentry around St Albans that might be persuaded to help fund the new church. He employed not ordinary 'begging' letters but finely lithographed appeals, some illustrated with line drawings, urging readers to give of 'the crumbs of your houses, your superfluity, your affluence, your luxury, in the name of my God for this poor beggar.' The idea was that the new church would be built by the rich and given to the poor. Quite overlooked was the generosity of Colney Heath people themselves to give of their utmost too. This they did, when the time came, with money and voluntary labour, for their own parish church.

From the day the first stone was laid, Nelson Dudding kept a paternal eye on the church at Colney Heath throughout his very long ministry at St Albans. He was over 84 years old when he celebrated his fiftieth year in office. He had preached his last sermon at St Peter's in 1886 when he was 78 but he continued to enjoy parsonage freehold and an active ministry until his death in 1895, aged 87.

This most remarkable of St Albans clergy ensured that a famous name continued. His second son was also named Horatio Nelson and he, too, entered the Navy and ended up an admiral!

The Revd Horatio Nelson Dudding lived an extraordinary life in extraordinary times. He achieved much in and around St Albans and time will continue to bear the fruit of his faithful ministry. In the family's burial plot, close to his parents' grave, Nelson Dudding is interred in St Peter's churchyard.

Save for the church itself, nowhere at Colney Heath is there to be seen a memorial honouring the founder of the parish.

Inset: *Horatio Nelson Dudding came to St Albans in 1842 from his first living at St Mary the Virgin, Stonham Parva, Suffolk.*

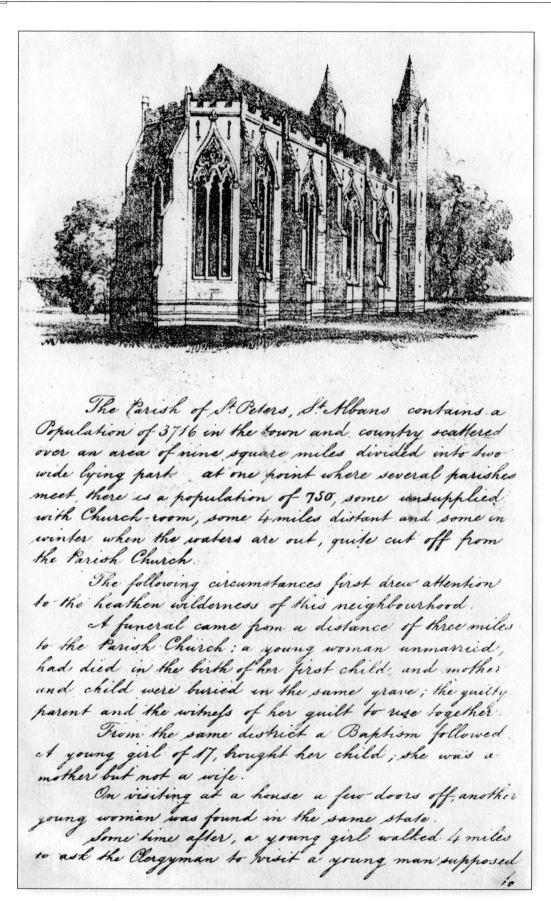

The Parish of St. Peters, St. Albans contains a Population of 3716 in the town and country scattered over an area of nine square miles divided into two wide lying part at one point where several parishes meet, there is a population of 750, some unsupplied with Church-room, some 4 miles distant and some in winter when the waters are out, quite cut off from the Parish Church.

The following circumstances first drew attention to the heathen wilderness of this neighbourhood.

A funeral came from a distance of three miles to the Parish Church: a young woman unmarried, had died in the birth of her first child and mother and child were buried in the same grave; the guilty parent and the witness of her guilt to use together.

From the same district a Baptism followed. A young girl of 17, brought her child; she was a mother but not a wife.

On visiting at a house a few doors off, another young woman was found in the same state.

Some time after, a young girl walked 4 miles to ask the Clergyman to visit a young man supposed

*The first appeal letter included a speculative design for a church for Colney Heath;
it drew in funds for the building finally agreed upon and consecrated in 1845.*

Chapter Two
Seeing Visions & Dreaming Dreams

Nelson Dudding's millenarian vision was clear. He wanted, as quickly as possible, a church for Colney Heath where faith could be taught and the Sacraments received. He knew from the start that the building would be simple, functional, perhaps even austere, and not comparable in any way with the glories of Stonham Parva. He shared with the later great Victorian church architect, Ninian Comper, the conviction that, on first entering, a church should bring a person to their knees. The building must 'move to worship and refresh man's soul in a weary land.'

While Nelson Dudding lacked a Comper or a Bodley designer, there was another member of the Nelson family – a cousin – who was an architect in the City of London Corporation, so he felt well placed to advance the cause so close to his heart. The cousin certainly played a part in the church design, most probably on the internal works while the external elevations are credited to another architect, Hugh Smith. The pace of what was to happen in the next two and a half years was truly remarkable. On his very first visit to Colney Heath to be apprised of the pastoral situation, Dudding noted that the opening of the High Street schoolroom for services on Sunday afternoons had been beneficial:

A paralysed and aged man was drawn by his son and neighbours more than a mile-and-a-half in a wheelchair to attend it. The window, door and stairs were thronged and, to use the words of a labouring man who was present: 'I counted nine score go out of the door.'

Painting a graphic picture of the 'heathen wilderness of this neighbourhood', the vicar of St Peter's told in his first appeal circular about the funeral of a young unmarried woman and her child buried in the same grave. He told of a 17-year-old who was 'a mother but not a wife', bringing her child for baptism, adding:

A young girl walked four miles to ask the clergyman to visit a man supposed to be dying:

'I am glad you are come. I lived like the rest; I passed the Sundays in drinking and riot. I lived like a beast and thought it was right to do so.' This was his own unasked confession. The mind is soon callous to sin.

Observing that Sunday morning was still the favourite time for prizefights in Colney Heath, Nelson Dudding told of his own experience visiting. One woman had been in the area for 30 years and another 38 years 'and had never seen a clergyman in their house before'.

By December 1842, Nelson Dudding had calculated that the place where the new church was needed contained a population of 750:

... some unsupplied with a church room, some four miles distant, and some, in winter when the waters are out, quite cut off from the parish church.

He continued:

What has the nation done to redeem this Wilderness? It has supplied beer shops in abundance, in which many spend their Sabbaths; and when the evil thus encouraged had grown up, it supplied for it the Police, the Treadmill and the Jail. There is a Lazarus lying at our gate full of sores. He desires to be fed with the crumbs which fall from the rich man's table. This Lazarus is a poor and neglected population far from the House of God, without the means of grace and without the Bread of Life or the Living Waters. Therefore, by moral and most certain consequences, from the crown of the head to the sole of the foot, he is full of sores.

Nelson Dudding probed St Peter's finances to reveal that the Great Tythes:

... which might do much for the parish are, by law, turned into other channels. The vicarial tythes are at present £270 a year, which though large compared with the stipend of many clergymen, will do little towards such demand.

He ended his plea:

A Corpse Way route out of Colney Heath.
Photo: Weston Marchant.

Thus this population has continued for centuries, and still is a monument of national guilt and an evidence of how much the Creatures of Eternity will do for time, how little for God. This effort is now made in the hope, that if successful, a church may be built large enough to contain 300 free sittings, and a resident clergyman, established in the centre of this district.

At the top of the lithographed appeal a perspective drawing shows a Gothic revival style church. The north-east view has the appearance of a public school's well-endowed chapel, with elaborate tracery in windows of two and three lancets, and intricate pinnacles. The main entrance was at the west end, finished off with two fanciful twin flanking towers. Allowing that the design was drawn up decades before any formal planning legislation and in a boldly imaginative style, it was hardly Hertfordshire: this prototype design was ruled out on the grounds of expense as the building materials alone were costed at just over £2000. While the original design was not pursued seriously for very long, nevertheless, it had a dramatic and stunning effect in the first of five circulars to go out about the proposed new church.

The second appeal, undated, but like all the publicity, was typeset by the St Albans printer, J.P.

Richardson, and contained a subscription list of 60 names with amounts of money given or pledged. Nelson Dudding summarised the appeal:

It pleased God so to bless that in the space of just one month a site for a chapel and sums sufficient to build it were promised. In dependence on the same blessing, and with a single view to His glory, a further appeal is now made to the charity of Christians to provide an endowment and a house for a resident clergyman.

As if to underline the need, the situation at Colney Heath was again highlighted:

In some instances, the moral condition of the people was found to be a heathen wilderness, under Christian responsibilities. Ignorance of God and of His ways, had brought the usual train of miseries, and sin multiplied upon sin: contempt of the Sabbath and ignorance of its duties – profaneness (sic) and immorality in their most degraded forms – men, women and children living and dying without God, and without hope.

This leaflet is signed also by the curate; the rector of Hatfield; the vicar of North Mymms; the incumbent of (London) Colney and by Edward Gibson, a St Albans solicitor, who was the appeal treasurer. These six plus a Mr J.S. Story of Bank, St Albans, and a Fleet Street, London address were to receive subscriptions for what was called St Peter's Chapel. A final line informs that Mr W. Joseph Bennett, a St Albans builder with a local yard 'has undertaken to build the chapel at prime cost'.

Sixteen of the cash donors in the published subscribers' list pledged sums in excess of £50. One was Robert William Gaussen, of Brookmans, whose substantial parkland to the east of Colney Heath, worked by Repton, was much later to become a commuters' suburb perpetuating the estate name. Robert Gaussen and his family owned a great deal of land in south Hertfordshire. His own mansion's grounds at North Mymms were extended in 1836 on the acquisition and demolition of nearby Gobions, a sixteenth-century house once the centre of a large estate belonging to the family of Sir Thomas More. Brookmans itself was destroyed by fire in 1891 and only the stables survive.

In addition to his personal cash donation, it was Robert Gaussen who gave the site for the church at Colney Heath. The land was identified in the Tithe Award of 1843 as a plot of land, one acre in extent. It was marked Smallford Chapel and described as 'part of a field or close of land called Hunger Hills'. This name can be traced back to the fifteenth century as 'Hungrel' which had been corrupted locally as 'Ungles'. The old name for Church Lane, before the church was built, was variously Hungerland or Ungles Lane. A modern house name nearby commemorates the old usage. The description 'Hunger Hill' was often given to any piece of land unrewarding to the farmer, so this gravelly area was aptly named. Its chief use had been to provide sand for spreading on cottage floors. In later years the part not appropriated for the church and extended churchyard was commercially quarried. The land on the shoulder could well be spared agriculturally and so it became 'God's Acre'.

BUILDING THE CHURCH

Preparations for building Colney Heath Church got under way in the winter of 1842–43 and gathered pace in the following spring and summer. Much of the early stage involved translating drawing-board plans into semi-reality in the builder's yard. The site had yet to be conveyed legally after passing, nominally at least, through the books of Her Majesty's Commissioners for Building New Churches, but it was never a Commissioners' church as such.

Dudding's third promotional leaflet – this time headed Colney Heath Chapel – noted that £1000 had been invested towards the endowment and, for the building itself, a further £1800 'at which sum the contract has been taken'. The subscription list increased from 60 to 141 names. Heading the donations from local and national benefactors were the wider Gaussen family's donations of £100, and from Tyttenhanger House the Countess of Caledon contributed £80.

Not forgotten by Nelson Dudding, on the final page, was 'the untiring and indefatigable zeal of an Association of Ladies'. Also acknowledged is the money collected in Colney Heath by local people – wheelwright, Charles Wilson, labourer James Franklin, Mrs Kenney; the School box; schoolmaster W. Gray, and one week's carting from George Stevenson. Further carting was by Messrs Arnold, Brown, Cannon, George, Gough, Knight, Pocock, Sworder, Tarry, Hart and William Wise. The vicar noted: 'rich and poor, farmer and labourer, have cheerfully given their aid and contributions.'

On-site building was well advanced by the spring of 1844. The conveyance was drawn up and invitations extended for 5 March to attend the ceremony 'for laying the first stone'. This formality, west of the north door, was performed by Robert Gaussen. The precise foundation block tapped into position is not identified; it may have been the low-set stone bearing on its face the mark of a trigonometry point. The silver trowel used by Gaussen at the ceremony is preserved. Hallmarked London 1829, it may be seen in the collection of St Albans Civic Plate: the ivory-handled tool bears the heraldic arms of St Albans on the obverse of the plain, pointed blade. Specially engraved on the reverse in honour of the occasion is the inscription:

FOR LAYING THE
FIRST STONE
OF
ST MARK'S CHURCH,
COLNEY HEATH,
ON THE 5TH DAY OF MARCH 1844
BY
R.W. GAUSSEN ESQ.
OF BROOKMANS

Two further engravings reveal that the trowel was first used at the stone-laying of St Albans Court

COLNEY HEATH CHAPEL,

ST. PETER'S,

ST. ALBAN'S.

THE success that has attended the above design, is, with unfeigned gratitude, ascribed to the Almighty God, in whose governance are the hearts of all mankind.

With His blessing, the exertions of various friends have so prospered this work of charity, commenced with the beginning of last year, that £1000. have been invested for an Endowment, and £1180. raised for the Building, at which sum the contract has been taken.

The presentation will be placed in the hands of three Trustees, of whom the Vicar of St. Peter's for the time will always be one, and the other two will act and fill up their own vacancies on certain principles in strict conformity with the articles of the Church of England.

The first stone will, it is hoped, be laid on the fifth of March next. The whole of the joiners' work, such as roof timber, floors, and pews, has been finished during the winter; and the stone work is in a forward state. Rich and poor, farmer and labourer, have cheerfully given their aid and contributions; which, together with the untiring and indefatigable zeal of an Association of Ladies, are thankfully acknowledged.

In subjoining an account of the Receipts, a hope is still cherished that by a continuance of effort a Parsonage House may be added to complete the design, as the locality of the Church nowhere offers a residence for a Clergyman's family.

The third promotional leaflet proclaims that £1000 had been invested for the endowment of the church with another £1800 raised for the building's construction. Notice was given of the foundation stone laying on 5 March 1844.

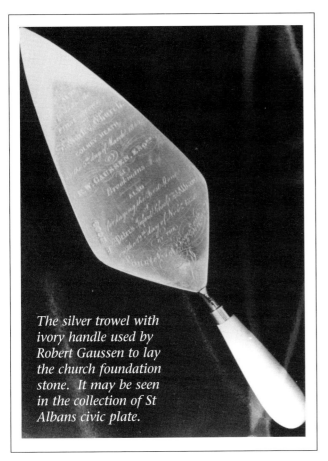

The silver trowel with ivory handle used by Robert Gaussen to lay the church foundation stone. It may be seen in the collection of St Albans civic plate.

House in August 1829 and subsequently by the Countess of Verulam, in November 1850, to set the foundation stone of St Peter's Infants School.

The invitation to the ceremony gave the first public indication that the dedication of the new church was to honour St Mark. This preference, making 25 April the church's patronal festival, was not too far from the day chosen for the stone laying: in any event a name had to go on the trowel and the invitations. St Mark the Evangelist was thought to be most appropriate.

Just prior to the ceremony, another appeal letter went out. It expressed Nelson Dudding's hope:

> *... still cherished that by a continuance of effort a Parsonage house may be added to complete the design, as the locality of the church nowhere offers a residence for a clergyman's family.*

By this time all the joinery work for the church – roof timbers, floors and pews – was ready and the stonework was in a 'forward state'. It was announced that the presentation to the living would be in the hands of three trustees who would 'act on certain principles in strict

The view through a coronet of trees to the parish church and its parsonage house of 1847.

COLNEY HEATH CHURCH.

The friends of Colney Heath Church are informed that it was opened for Divine Service by License from the Bishop, on Sunday, June 15th, and will be Consecrated in due time. A Population of 800 surrounds it, and a Clergyman is resident among them. There are Two full Services on a Sunday, and a Lecture in the Week: 120 Children in the School with an efficient Schoolmaster: about 30 Communicants attended the first Communion. An accurate judgement cannot yet be formed of the Congregation, as the novelty still attracts; but 640 have issued from a Church built for 350. It is an enclosure for the Lord, in what was once a wilderness.

To continue the advantages of a resident Ministry, another effort must still be made for a Parsonage House and Endowment. No public Charity will contribute any help. The Clergyman who receives the £30 a year, the interest of £1000 already invested, is compelled to pay £40 for his Lodgings in the only available House to be found.

So much has been contributed, and so liberally, that, with this statement, the case is left to such as are able to make a final effort for the completion of this work of God.

St. Albans,
July, 1845.

There was good news in Nelson Dudding's fourth public letter, dated July 1845, about attendances at the completed church as well as at the Sunday school. However, more funds were needed for a parsonage house.

conformity with the Articles of the Church of England.' The church, designed to seat 350, was licensed and came into use on Sunday, 15 June 1845, prior to being consecrated 'in due time'. Nelson Dudding noted in his fourth letter, dated July 1845 and headed Colney Heath Church:

A population of 800 surrounds the church and a clergyman is resident among them. There are two full services on a Sunday and a lecture in the week: 120 children in the school with an efficient schoolmaster. About 30 communicants attended the first communion. An accurate judgement cannot yet be formed of the congregation as the novelty still attracts, but 640 have issued from a church built for 350. It is an enclosure for the Lord in what was once a wilderness. To continue

the advantages of a resident ministry, another effort must still be made for a Parsonage house and Endowment. No public charity will contribute any help.

Here was a real problem. Mr Dudding's curate at Colney Heath received the going rate of £30 a year – the interest on the £1000 invested – but, as the vicar pointed out in the manner of Mr Micawber:

He is compelled to pay £40 for his lodgings in the only available house to be found. So much has been contributed, and so liberally, that with this statement the case is left to such as are able to make a final effort for the completion of this work of God.

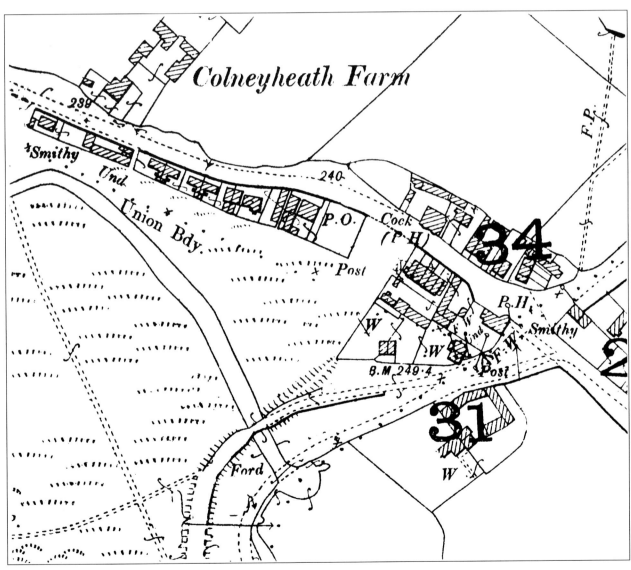

The centre of the village around the Cock and the Queen's Head public houses. This map of 1898 shows there was a Post Office and two blacksmiths; the water supply is marked by the location of wells (W). The river crossing is shown as a ford. Reproduced from the 1898 Ordnance Survey map.

Attached to the letter was a list of 45 donors who had contributed £859 towards the clergy house and endowment.

The packed first service, with Holy Communion, has its detail preserved on printed cards handed to the congregation. The front carried a prayer for the 'Blessing of God on Colney Heath Church'. On the reverse were the words of the hymn, 'Come, Holy Ghost, our souls inspire', which would have been sung unaccompanied as provision of a hand-pumped organ was not an early priority for the new church.

Between the licensing and the consecration, eventually fixed for the end of December, Nelson Dudding published the final accounts: there had been no borrowing from a bank, and no private loans had been taken out. The accounts reveal that total receipts were £2564.5s.½d. The builder was paid £1058.6s.2½d. for his work. This did not include certain special expenses such as costs for 'bricks and cartage', alterations and the architect's fee – £66.5s.6d. When a sum of 17s.2½d. was added for 'extra weight' for the bell – of half a hundred-weight, 19½ inches and inscribed C. & G. Mears, Founders, London 1844 – the final certificated expenditure came to £1457.6s.6½d.

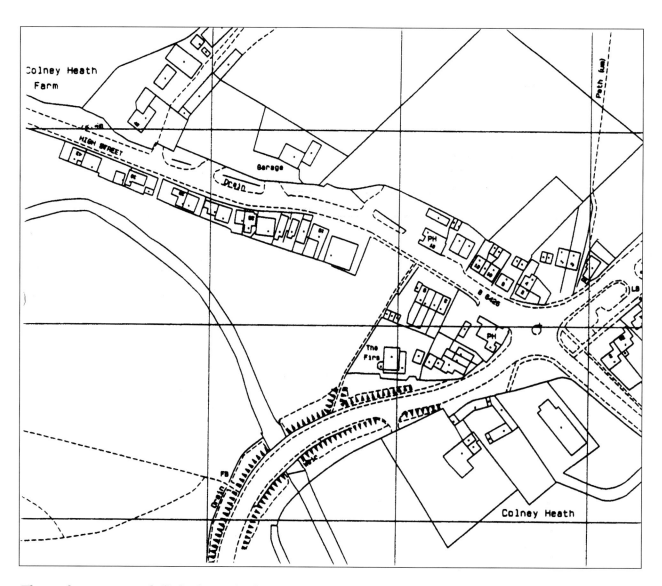

The modern map reveals little change in the total number of properties. Development north-west of the road junction includes the building once used as Colney Heath's manually-operated telephone exchange, now a dwelling. Reproduced from the 2001 Ordnance Survey 1:2500 digital data map. © Crown copyright.

THE REV. H. N. DUDDING, AND MR. EDWARD GIBSON,

IN ACCOUNT WITH

The Committee for Building a New Church

AT

ST. PETER'S, ST. ALBANS.

RECEIPTS.	£.	s.	d.
Amount of Subscriptions received ..	1927	18	6
One Year and half's Dividend on £1059. 12s. 3d. Consols.......	45	8	7
Amount Collected by the Ladies' Association at St. Albans	433	19	4
Balance due to the Treasurers	156	18	7½
£	2564	5	0½

PAYMENTS.	£.	s.	d.
Paid Builder, as per Contract for Building Church	1058	6	2½
Ditto, for Fencing round Church Yard	43	7	5
Bricklayers' and other Bills for Alterations ordered by Architect	10	2	10
Extra Weight for Bell...........		17	2½
Architect's Commission and Expences	66	5	6
Invested in the Consols, for an Endowment Fund	1000	0	0
For Printing Cards.............	4	14	6
For Power of Attorney, to receive Dividends	1	1	6
Paid for Bricks, Carting, and Tolls	321	14	9½
Richardson, for Printing	2	11	0
Mr. Gaussen's Solicitors, their Charges for furnishing Abstract of Title, &c......	8	0	0
Paid Labourer's Levelling Church Yard, and making Fences	8	18	11
For Advertisements.............	3	3	0
Sundry Disbursements for Stationery, Postages and Porterage paid by Rev. H. N. Dudding..	9	6	6
Paid Agent's Charges for Office Copies, Wills, &c. required by the Solicitor to the Church Commissioners, &c. and for Counsel's Fees for preparing Trust Deed	13	5	5
Sundry Disbursements for Stationery, Postages, Carriage of Parcels, and Money expended by Mr. Gibson.............	5	13	3
£	2564	5	0½

The completed accounts as produced by Horatio Nelson Dudding.
Expenditure included the sum of £43.7s.5d. for fencing the churchyard.

THE CONSECRATION

Without doubt, the consecration of St Mark's Church on Tuesday, 30 December 1845 was the most eagerly awaited and splendid occasion in the life of Colney Heath. People were consumed with excitement at the prospect of seeing a bishop in the village. In fact, this most rural outpost of the Anglican Church belonged to the huge Diocese of London and was to be embraced by the man at its head – the third most senior figure in the Church of England – the Rt Revd and Rt Hon. Charles James Blomfield, Lord Bishop of London. Delight about the visit was widespread. The only surprise was over the rather unexpected and slightly inconvenient date between Christmas and the new year: there was a reason for it.

The people of Colney Heath plus 'several of the nobility and gentry of the neighbourhood' began arriving early for the 11.30am service. They clutched numbered admission tickets with instructions on the reverse advising where carriages and horses should be left. It mattered not that it was raining heavily.

The carriage bringing the Bishop of London to Colney Heath arrived punctually, something Charles Blomfield had guaranteed by travelling to Hertfordshire the previous day in order to stay overnight at his brother's house at Stevenage. Thus he ensured a more comfortable journey on the morning of the ceremony as well as avoiding rising much earlier which would have been necessary had he set out from his official residence, Fulham Palace.

Excitement mounted as in black frock-coat, breeches and gaiters, the prelate, more accustomed to presiding at magnificent and well-ordered liturgy in the splendour of St Paul's Cathedral, alighted from his carriage in Ungles Lane. He was met by senior clergy, the vicar of St Peter's and the parish churchwardens. Some 38 visiting clergy led a procession and packed into the front pews of the church for the consecration which began with Morning Prayer. Every detail of the service was recorded in the Bishop of London's records, hand-written by the diocesan registrar: the record is preserved in the City of London Guildhall library. Four days after the ceremony a glowing report appeared in the columns of *John Bull*, whose 16 pages of society news for the price of 6d. was expensive at the time.

Before entering the church for the service, the bishop, by this time in Convocation robes, processed round the churchyard perimeter to define the consecrated curtilage and dedicate the land intended for burials. Not all the land given by Gaussen was required for the church and churchyard; an area was earmarked for glebe and the future parsonage. The house was to have its own driveway that lead off a carriage road.

As well as setting out the consecration rite, the diocesan registrar's manuscript refers to various deeds, trusts and declarations. Registrar J.N. Shephard began his report by noting: 'The church was filled up with pews and seats and furnished with all things necessary and proper for the celebration of Divine Worship.'

There is a complete record of the Bible readings, psalm, and even of the hymns sung: the occasion predated the first edition of *Hymns Ancient and Modern* (1861).

The Bishop of London was the celebrant at Holy Communion in the shallow apsidal sanctuary. Ready on the communion table, set

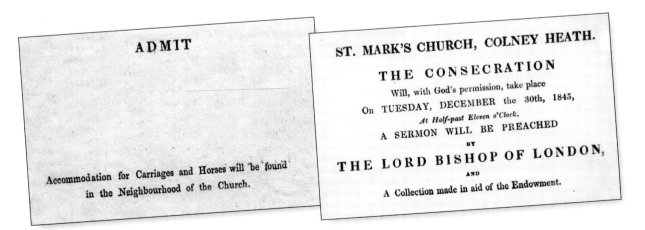

ADMIT

Accommodation for Carriages and Horses will be found in the Neighbourhood of the Church.

ST. MARK'S CHURCH, COLNEY HEATH.

THE CONSECRATION

Will, with God's permission, take place

On TUESDAY, DECEMBER the 30th, 1845,

At Half-past Eleven o'Clock.

A SERMON WILL BE PREACHED

BY

THE LORD BISHOP OF LONDON,

AND

A Collection made in aid of the Endowment.

Admission tickets were prepared for the consecration of St Mark's; the tickets were numbered on the reverse. There must have been quite a traffic jam of carriages and horses with parking and stabling problems.

The road from Colney Heath Lane in front of the church. The 36 new houses at Wistlea Crescent had been built across the road.

with a white linen cloth, was the church plate; the new pieces shone brightly among gifted vessels of mellow, older provenance. Above, pale morning light made translucent the polished plain quarries and 'cathedral' glass in the round-headed lancets of the east window. Hushed whispers in the pews gave way to silence. White breath upon the cold air combined to hold the whole assembly still, as if fixed for a moment in some great historic tapestry. It was a unique, precious scene within the Christmas festival: led by the chief pastor of the diocese, the time had come to celebrate again the holy mysteries.

At the start of the consecration the bishop offered a prayer for the special occasion:

Blessed be Thy name, O Lord God, for that it pleaseth Thee to have Thy habitation among the Sons of Men upon earth. Bless, we beseech Thee, the religious solemnity of this day; and grant that in this place, now set apart to Thy service, Thy Holy Name may be worshipped in truth and purity to all generations, through Jesus Christ our Lord. Amen.

Those attending the consecration could see for themselves the modest furnishings provided in the church. There was somewhere to preach from – 'His Lordship ascended the pulpit and preached a most excellent and appropriate sermon.' His text was St Matthew ch.11 v. 5: 'The poor have the Gospel preached to them.' Poor or not, the congregation contributed nearly £100 to the collection.

Nelson Dudding plus the rector of Hatfield and the vicar of North Mymms were the first trustees of St Mark's. A vacancy among them would be filled by nomination of the remaining two, the qualification to serve being simply having a living within 15 miles of St Peter's, St Albans.

The trust deed presented at the consecration provided that of the 350 seats '117 of such sittings shall be and continue for ever as Free Sittings.' Until ratification of the new parish by the Privy Council and election of churchwardens, the income from the remaining pew rents was to be apportioned by the trustees in whose hands the advowson was gifted. Part of the rents would go towards 'paying the salary of the clerk, beadles, pew openers and other expenses incident to the performance of Divine Service in the new church.'

Following the service the bishop took his carriage to Oaklands, the country house of William Knight. The estate of 315 acres to the east of St Albans was described as having 'matured pleasure gardens and a well-timbered park'. The Georgian mansion of 1782 had been romantically converted with Tudor trim and a castellated tower was added in 1844. Set back off the Hatfield Road, Oaklands stood in splendid isolation. As late as 1919 there was not a single house between Beaumont Avenue and the south lodge of Oaklands. The estate became an agricultural college in September 1921, opening with 17 students.

35

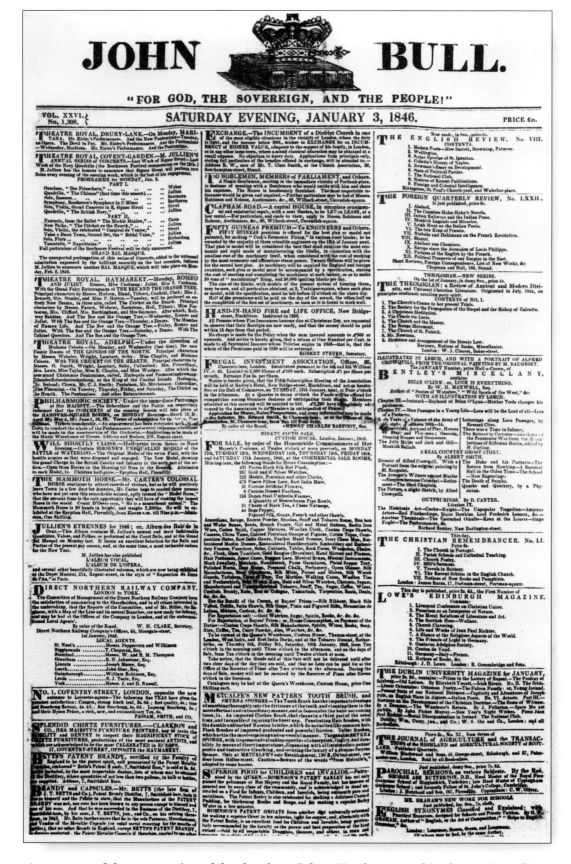

An account of the consecration of the church at Colney Heath appeared in the evening edition of the society paper, John Bull, *on Saturday 3 January 1846. The paper would have had little following in Colney Heath and, at 6d., would have been considered an expensive luxury.*

The early understated interior of St Mark's Church is said to have been 'furnished with all things necessary'.

The larger of the gifted chalices in the church plate appears to be hallmarked 1742, while the pedestal paten is dated 1701. The older flagon, 10½" high, bears the date 1842 with a hallmark stamp showing the head of the young Queen Victoria. The two smaller patens, the small flagon and a silver box for unconsecrated communion elements are of relatively later provenance.

Inside, at the reception and luncheon following the consecration service 'everything was provided with the most sumptuous liberality.' The large turnout of clergy honoured the bishop, showed support for the new church and for Nelson Dudding's efforts, but it was motivated also by reasons of more than passing red-letter day significance. The memorable visitation to the parish was the first and last duty performed by the Rt Revd Charles Blomfield as its bishop. The very next day, when the bishop awoke after staying the night at Oaklands, the new parish along with most of Hertfordshire and much more, had ceased to be part of the Diocese of London. The whole ecclesiastical area was transferred from Blomfield's See and – inexplicably, or so it seemed – put in with Kent as part of the Diocese of Rochester!

In 1845 the London Diocese sprawled into the remote rural territory of the northern Home Counties. It included all of Essex and most of Hertfordshire, making it seem peculiar for the Bishop of London to have oversight of both Hitchin and Harwich. Blomfield's plan was to exchange the distant villages of Essex and Hertfordshire for nearer boroughs south of the Thames. The South-Bank communities were undeniably London, but hitherto, were strangely dispersed among three dioceses – Winchester, Rochester and Canterbury.

Left: In 1867 Thomas Legh Claughton, a former vicar of Kidderminster, became the 96th Bishop of Rochester and, therefore, just two days after the consecration of St Mark's, he had the church in his charge when the new parish was transferred from the London Diocese. Claughton was translated in 1877 as the first Bishop of the new Diocese of St Albans.

The East Drive of Oaklands, seat of William Knight, who put on the reception and luncheon for the Bishop of London following the consecration of Colney Heath Church. This secondary driveway, beginning off Oaklands Lane, Smallford, is closely planted with chestnut trees, seen here as young saplings.

SEEING VISIONS & DREAMING DREAMS

Depriving Rochester of South London meant that diocese was left with just its city and deanery, hence the stop-gap measure of adding territory from north of the Thames was put in place. It was a clumsy arrangement. Blomfield offloaded Essex and the Archdeaconry of St Albans at midnight on New Year's Eve 1845, the day following St Mark's consecration. The people had seen a high-ranking prelate for the first time: it was the first and last time that a Bishop of London was to set buckled-shoe foot in Colney Heath.

Anyone present at the consecration that anticipated the splendour of Wren's masterpiece, St Paul's, as their cathedral had only one more day to relish the thought. Despite the fact that the first Archbishop of Canterbury had simultaneously founded the Sees of London and Rochester, it was going to be difficult for Colney Heath people to love a dilapidated mother church in Kent, let alone get to their cathedral easily or at all.

Some 440 clergymen from Hertfordshire and Essex sent Bishop Blomfield messages expressing regret at their loss of connection with him and the Diocese of London; Blomfield retired in 1865. It would, of course, have been impossible, in the circumstances, for the Bishop of Rochester to remain beyond the Medway at Bishopscourt. A palace was found for him, rather inaccessibly too, at Danbury near Chelmsford. The village, at 365ft above sea level, is at the highest point in Essex.

It was left to the much-loved vicar of Kidderminster to move mountains. On 11 June 1867, the vicar, Thomas Legh Claughton, was consecrated the 96th Bishop of Rochester. From Danbury he soon had his eyes on the ancient Abbey Church of St Albans – then a parish church – as an alternative seat for his diocese or as the cathedral at the heart of an entirely new diocese. It took until March 1875 to get the Bishopric of St Albans Bill through Parliament. Claughton was translated to St Albans and, on 12 June 1877, enthroned in the Abbey as the first bishop. Colney Heath was to welcome seven more bishops in its first 150 years as a parish.

In becoming part of the new See of St Albans, the church at Colney Heath had entered its third diocese. Its vicar was the man who had started the ministry in the village 32 years earlier, the Revd George Frederick Williamson, who in 1877 was six years into a second incumbency at St Mark's; he remained in post until October 1880.

COLNEY HEATH, HERTS.—Tuesday being appointed for the consecration of St. Mark's Church, notwithstanding the unfavourable state of the weather the Church was well filled, including several of the nobility and gentry of the neighbourhood. The Lord Bishop of London, who slept at his brother's at Stevenage, arrived punctually at half-past eleven o'clock, and was received by a large body of the Clergy, the Minister of St. Peter's, the Churchwardens, &c. The usual service of the day was commenced by the Vicar of St. Peter's reading the prayers, and the Incumbent of Colney Heath the Lessons. The Communion Service was read by the Bishop and his Chaplain; after which his Lordship ascended the pulpit, and preached a most excellent and appropriate sermon from the Gospel of St. Mathew, chap. xi., v. 5: "The poor have the Gospel preached to them."—A collection was made while the Offertory was being read, and the proceeds delivered to the Bishop, who laid them on the Communion table—the amount being nearly 100l. After the termination of the service, the Bishop proceeded to Oatlands, the seat of William Knight, Esq. About 38 of the Clergy were present, and it is needless to add that everything was provided with the most sumptuous liberality. The Right Rev. Prelate's health was drunk with the warmest expressions of affection and respect. In a word, everything passed off with the highest satisfaction to all concerned in the proceedings of the day.

The report of the consecration of St Mark's as it appeared in John Bull *four days after the service.*

The Gothic revival style church ruled out as too expensive for Colney Heath, at £2000.
The drawing, however, inspired fund-raising for what was eventually built.

The architect's sketch of the north and west elevations of the finally approved building.
A clock was clearly anticipated but the circular driveway did not materialise.

Chapter Three
A New Year & A New Beginning

'LOVERS OF BEAUTY WITHOUT EXTRAVAGANCE'

New Year's Day 1846 marked a great new beginning for Colney Heath. The new church, two days after consecration and transfer to its second diocese, was ready for ministry and mission. The building looked resplendent in the pristine brightness of yellow London brick with quoins and Bath stone dressing. The Byzantine style distinguished the little hillock it graced, giving sudden diminished scale to the huddle of little cottages to its north-west. The church was inviting and it made welcome a large number of sightseers as well as a regular congregation.

Passing beyond the fat stone columns of the north porch, worshippers entering the church found a plainness suggesting an exaggerated spaciousness in the single-cell building. The nave, which was without an aisle, led eastward, not to a chancel but straight to the vestigial sanctuary, up one step, and set within a shallow apse. Pitch-pine pews were 'set solid' coming to within a short distance of the communion rail. To the north and south sides of the sanctuary was just room enough for the clergy reading desk and the pulpit. The upright seating for the congregation reached back to the west end where the large font

A row of little cottages with dormer windows once stood west of the church.

occupied the space between the two ranks of pews. Above, supported by slender columns, the thin gallery set off the large west window, and its tiered seating offered considerable 'overflow' accommodation. The space-consuming organ console and casing did not appear for another 42 years.

The simple interior was planned by Nelson Dudding in order that the church might not easily be 'Newmanised'. The time was one of intense debate about the direction of the Church of England. John Henry Newman (1801–90) was prominent in the newly formed Oxford Movement, dedicated to the sacramental elements in religious tradition and to reforming the Church. Newman was received into the Roman Catholic Church in October 1845 and became a cardinal in 1879.

Nelson Dudding was concerned, also, about the possibility of the patronage of his St Albans living, then with the Bishop of Ely, passing back to the Crown. He feared the presentation coming under the Oxford Movement's influence: it was a thought he did not relish even at the start of his 52-year ministry in St Albans. For that reason he did not bind his successors, automatically, to being

among the three trustees of Colney Heath Church. The chosen three were bound to apply seven trusteeship principles reflecting the 39 Articles: the rule has been applied consistently in the appointment of incumbents from the beginning.

So the church took its place in a community far removed from the modern concepts of the hypermarket, the Internet and e-mail. Roads continued to be dust tracks; there were no cars, no trains and it was to be another 30 years before the telephone was invented.

The living started as a perpetual curacy and continued as such for some years, even after independent parish status was granted. There was an intriguing diversion as a result of the District Church Tithes Act 1865 which provided for perpetual curacy benefices to be constituted rectories. This option, although investigated and held as a possibility, failed to achieve legal confirmation at Colney Heath.

The progress of St Mark's is best related to the years in office served by the clergy appointed to the living. In total, 12 priests have served 13 incumbencies in 150 years of remarkable development in both church and parish.

The apsidal east elevation of the church and the little vestry on the south-east corner.

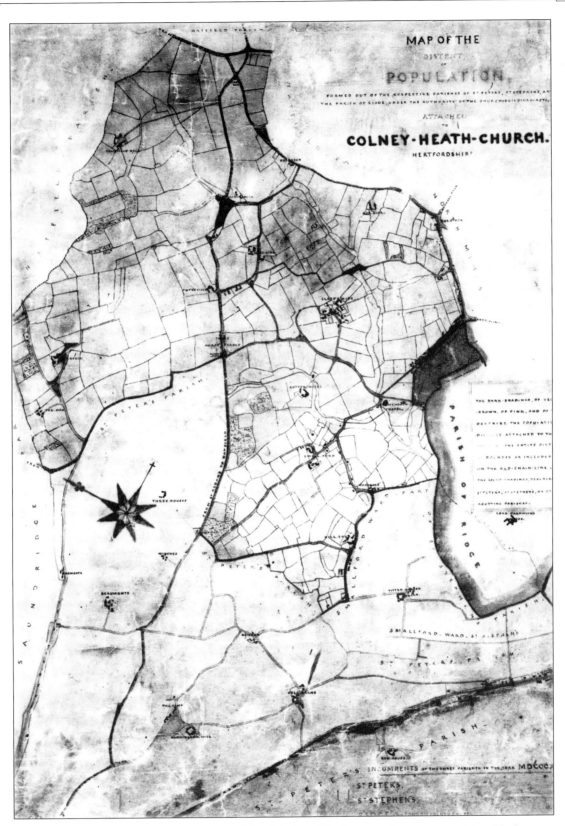

When it came into being, the new parish of Colney Heath served an area considerably larger than it does today. This 'population' map was prepared in 1844. From the north, the parish extended beyond Fiddle Bar to the edge of Hatfield Park, then to Hill End on the west. 'North corner' was beyond Beech Farm and Colney Heath Common is the shaded area on the south-eastern boundary; next to it can be seen the open triangle bounded by the High Street, Church Lane and Park Lane and the church site.

Twelve Clergy in 150 Years

The 13 incumbencies, with dates of priests' appointment, licensing or institution and induction are:

[1]1845	15 June	George Frederick Williamson
1847	22 February	James Boucher
1847	14 September	Thomas Jenison Cuffe
1850	18 October	William Roche
1871	17 November	George Frederick Williamson (second term)
1880	20 November	William Bailey
1898	5 April	Laurence George Bomford
1918	22 December	John Browne Ost
1926	26 May	Albert Marchant
[2]1933	26 January	George Weston Byers-Jones
[3]1954	18 May	Ross McPherson Heard
1958	24 June	William Edwin Butland
[4]1980	1 December	David Roger Veness

NOTES

[1]Some documents date the first incumbency from December 1846 when St Mark's was made a separate ecclesiastical district. Williamson was appointed when the church opened in June 1845. He served two incumbencies at Colney Heath, with 24 years between them.

[2]In July 1952, on the retirement of George Byers-Jones, a Presentation Suspension Order was made by the bishop. The Revd Canon F.G. Brenchley, vicar of St Paul's, St Alban's, was also put in charge of St Mark's. In the three months immediately prior to the appointment of the Revd Ross McPherson Heard, the Revd Charles Lawrence, appointed to a new church, St Michael' and All Angel's at Boreham Wood, took some of the services at Colney Heath while living, pro tem, at the vicarage.

[3]In February 1958 a second presentation suspension of just three months was imposed until the Revd W.E. Butland was licensed as curate-in-charge in the following June. He was instituted as vicar a year later.

[4]The Revd D.R. Veness resigned the living in March 1998.

THE PARSONAGE HOUSE

When Nelson Dudding appealed for funds to build a clergy house at Colney Heath he was thinking of something less grand than his own vicarage in St Albans. The village parsonage house, to be set to the south-west of the church, needed to be a home adequate for a country clergyman, his wife and family and large enough for modest entertaining but not ostentatious. Dudding thought the £858 raised for the purpose, less a contribution towards the endowment, would do nicely.

The new house, eventually completed two years after the church, turned out to be the largest to be seen in Colney Heath. Variously called the Parsonage, the Rectory and the Vicarage, the brick building under a slated roof exactly captured the style of the age. It graced one rood and 23 poles of land, including glebe, conveyed in July 1846, and the house was ready for Thomas Jenison Cuffe and his wife to move in as the first occupiers in 1847.

An ample outer north porch led to a large reception hall with access to the drawing room, dining room, study and kitchen, the latter leading to the scullery and pantry. There was also a large ground-floor utility room. Upstairs arrangements provided for seven bedrooms plus a box room; one of these was described as 'maid's bedroom' and another 'maid's room'. Open fires provided heating while lighting was achieved through use of oil lamps. There was great excitement in 1932 when the oil lamps were discarded in favour of electric lighting. Some 22 points and switches were needed, which, with bulbs – including two each for the study and the 'best bedroom' – cost £17.10s. fitted.

Outside, the promised carriage drive was provided, joining the road near a water-splash, later to be bridged. At the head of the drive, at right angles to the vicarage, was a coach house. This commodious place had a fitted rail with pegs to take six sets of harnesses, bridles and saddles. Nearby was a large iron storage tank, a timber-built workshop, a greenhouse with fitted shelving and a large water butt.

At the end of his 20-year incumbency, Laurence Bomford (1898–1918) made a detailed inventory of the fittings and fixtures in every room, down to the 37 hooks for cups on the seven-foot deal dresser in the pantry. He estimated the value at £51.11s. for all the contents.

Vicarage garden parties were a favourite pastime. The garden was the children's paradise; they loved exploring the network of paths into the copse on the south side. There was the formal part set with flower beds and borders, a shrubbery to screen the churchyard and a large lawn. This was pure Barsetshire; it could easily have been Trollope's *Framley Parsonage*. Finding gardeners to keep up with the grounds' maintenance was possible but their task was enormous. Gradually the formal flower beds gave way to more shrubs, grass and organised wilderness. When the new vicarage was built in 1972, effectively on part of the front garden of the original one, it seemed to make little impact upon the spaciousness that had previously existed.

The various methods employed to heat the first house were never very successful. Over the years, in order to conserve heat and running costs, clergy occupiers and their families retreated to fewer rooms, often employing auxiliary means of heating at their own expense. The work went on with remarkably few complaints despite the cold and damp, draughty windows and doors, condensation and leaks. Vicarage families survived. By and large, incumbents, their wives and a succession of apple-cheeked children recall only happy times when home was Colney Heath Vicarage. The twelfth incumbent, W.E. Butland (1958–80) and his family were the last to occupy the old house which was sold to the Christian youth organisation, The Campaigners. The Butlands rejoiced at their good fortune the day St Albans Diocesan Parsonages Board undertook to provide a new, modern, purpose-built vicarage. More manageable arrangements enabled garden parties to flourish once more with occasional summer Sunday luncheon parties after church for congregational families.

The parsonage of 1847 became the largest house to be seen in Colney Heath. It was built at a cost of £850.

The south face of the benefice house, often bathed in bright sunlight, overlooked the formal gardens and copse.

The Parkgate Corner entrance to Colney Heath common.

The Revd George Frederick Williamson
Curate-in-Charge, June 1845–February 1847. Vicar, November 1871–October 1880

The first Anglican clergyman to come to Colney Heath served two separate terms of office. He was the careful choice of Horatio Nelson Dudding and had been groomed for the job from the days when the church was simply lines on the drawing board.

George Williamson, an MA of Trinity College, Cambridge, had a lean time in the village during his first stay as renting a house had left him out of pocket. Despite the difficulties, he set the tone for years to come, and, feeling sufficiently encouraged, he returned in 1871 for a second term, by then enjoying the comforts of the parsonage and continuing in office as vicar for a further nine years.

By the end of his first year, Williamson saw the church centred on a new ecclesiastical district. He was involved in a number of firsts for the church: he officiated at the first interment in the churchyard, obligingly turning out on Boxing Day 1846 to conduct the funeral of Sarah Day, aged 70. In total, the burial book records 800 funerals up to the book's completion on 28 February 1911.

He conducted the first baptism at Colney Heath. For this initiation the stone font of St Mark's waited for its own until 31 January 1847, courtesy of Levi, the infant son of George and Susan Reynolds, born on 7 December 1846. Baptisms were keenly sought as the population began to grow. It took only until January 1879 to complete the first baptismal book of 800 entries.

A singular honour fell to Williamson during his second term at Colney Heath. In 1874 he was party to what was intended to be a well-kept secret involving his guide and mentor, Horatio Nelson Dudding. Various references appear in St Mark's archives to the effect that 'in his old age' the founder of the church, then widowed, married again, going secretly to Colney Heath for the ceremony.

The man who pleaded the cause of St Mark's back in 1842 was married the second time at Colney Heath. No marriage banns were called there, nor were they called by the St Peter's vicar himself in his own church. Nelson Dudding and his bride-to-be, Esther Hope, spinster of St Peter's parish, wished the ceremony to be a private affair. The reading of banns would have made their intentions prematurely known. They chose the less public option of obtaining a superintendent registrar's certificate.

Despite past incumbents' annotated remarks regarding this marriage such as 'this must be checked', nobody appears to have done so. The writer found the wedding of Nelson Dudding and Esther Hope took place at St Mark's on 27 August 1874, the detail being confirmed in the register entry. On the wedding day, Nelson Dudding, then aged 66, and Esther Hope, set out from St Albans, each taking a different route to Colney Heath to avoid giving away any clues. While Williamson was conducting the marriage ceremony at St Mark's, the verger back at St Peter's had discovered what was going on and, to the irritation of Nelson Dudding's family, ran up the Union flag on St Peter's tower as part of the day's eventual widespread rejoicings.

Throughout his second incumbency Williamson followed his predecessor's usage by describing and signing himself, Rector. Doubtless, he believed he was entitled to the style despite the near proximity of his clerical mentor who might have apprised him otherwise.

George Williamson resigned from his second tenure at Colney Heath on 27 October 1880; he died in March 1900, aged 81. There is no memorial to him at the church.

Inset: *Hundreds of infants came for baptism at the original font at St Mark's. Levi Reynolds was the first, on the last day of January 1847.*

*An early photograph of Bell Lane
(Coursers Road) skirting a flooded common.*

The church from the north-east.

Chapter Four

The Early Years: Up to 1880

SCATTERED COMMUNITIES

Incumbents of the new parish found they had to journey much farther afield than the village of Colney Heath. Over the years the original parish boundaries have been adjusted several times. Initially, the parish extended from Fiddle Bar at Hatfield to Hill End in the west. What was called North Corner lay beyond Beech Farm, while Colney Heath Common was at the southern boundary. Originally the parish did not extend eastward beyond Roestock Lane where it met with the parish of North Mymms. Inaccessible locations for clergy in the early days included Wilkins Green, Roe Green, Ellenbrooke and the area of Harpsfield, later consumed by Hatfield airfield.

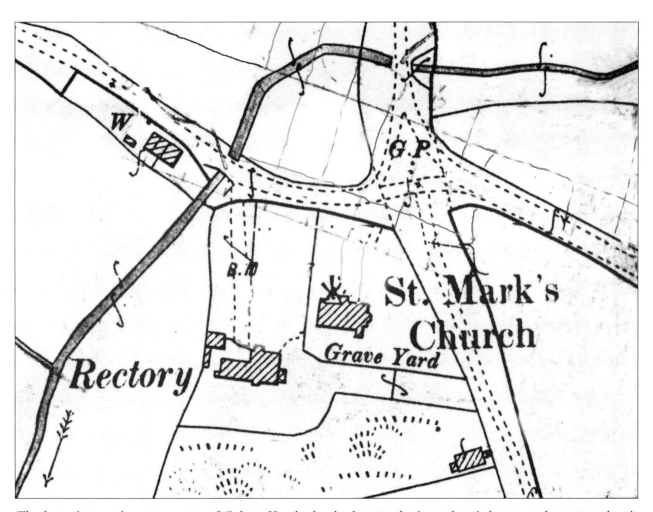

The late-nineteenth-century map of Colney Heath clearly denotes the incumbent's home as the rectory, but it never was. Close to Church Lane may be seen the first of the parish halls – the Iron Room.
Reproduced from the 1898 Ordnance Survey map.

The Revd James Boucher
Curate-in-Charge, February – September 1847

The stay of James Boucher was the shortest of all the clergy to hold office at Colney Heath. He was in post for just seven months during 1847, the year the parsonage house was completed.

The new parsonage, with specifications approved by Nelson Dudding, was ready before the end of the year but, no doubt, slow progress in the building works dispirited the young curate and spurred him to move on quickly.

No baptisms or marriages are recorded in Boucher's time at Colney Heath. The burial register confirms he did conduct three funerals as officiating minister.

The year 1847 marked the publication by the Revd W. Upton, minister of St Albans Baptist Church, of his work, *Survey of Religion in Hertfordshire*. In it he frankly assesses the 'character of ministry' locally:

St Michael (St Albans)	*Rector: aged and laid aside*
	Curate: pompous and unevangelical
Temperance Chapel (St Albans)	*Teetotalism and little else*
St Peter (St Albans)	*Dudding: Pious, evangelical, millenarian*
	Curate: less decided

A little later, in 1851, came an enquiring Religious Census. The aim of this, together with the Upton report, was to ascertain the quantity of accommodation provided for worship and what proportion of the population attended church or chapel. Additionally, the survey probed and evaluated the quality of preaching in each community. Comments from the clergy themselves and church officers cover a multitude of subjects including finance, pews, weather and illness. It makes the modern Archdeacon's Visitation questions appear very mild.

Gathering storm clouds above the Mill House.
Photo: Weston Marchant

The view towards The Warren with Colney Heath Mill beyond. Pen-and-ink study by Roger Zucca.

The Revd Thomas Jenison Cuffe
Curate-in-Charge, September 1847–September 1850

Ministering for just short of three years, Thomas Cuffe, aged 50, when he arrived, conducted the first marriage service in St Mark's: this was between Frederick Pratt and Emma Sprigings, both described in the register as 'servant'.

Cuffe's wife, Frances, appeared regularly at church weddings. She was happy to leave the new parsonage to join the congregation for the ceremony and be on hand to sign the register as witness. This was a regular routine, owing not a little to convenience and more to the necessity to find people who could provide a signature. Occasionally, in the first marriage register, couples penned a cross, leaving the officiating minister to add 'his mark' or 'her mark'.

Thomas Cuffe had a Bachelor of Arts degree: he was keen on education for the people. In his time the average daily attendance at the schoolroom remained around 80, while numbers at the Sunday school continued to rise to a peak of 120. During this time, St Mark's was described as 'the parish church' or 'the district church'. A religious service was conducted in the schoolroom on Sunday evening either by Cuffe or Mr Gray, the schoolmaster. There is no memorial to Thomas Cuffe at Colney Heath.

Colney Heath secured a good write-up in the Upton Report with church attendance noted at 200 'at fullest'. Cuffe, as occupant of the parsonage, was described as evangelical and active.

The Revd William Roche
Priest-in-Charge, October 1850–1871

William Roche completed a little over 21 years and seven months at Colney Heath. His death, on 11 August 1871 at the age of 63 made him the first of three incumbents to die in office.

Incumbent is the most appropriate description for Mr Roche who variously identified himself by a variety of styles. The living in 1850 was a perpetual curacy still and William Roche was not enamoured. He quickly set about a voluminous correspondence – with the erudite pen of an MA of Christ Church, Oxford – to take advantage of a peculiar piece of legislation providing for perpetual curacy benefices to be made either vicarial or rectorial. He had placed his aspirations on the District Church Tithes Act 1865, a formula rich in Victorian compromise which might have been invented for the benefit of Gilbert and Sullivan. Clearly, the incumbent was intent on becoming the rector of Colney Heath: his campaign to effect the translation was intriguing, to say the least, but it turned out to be a case of championing a lost cause.

London-born William Roche was 42 when he moved to Colney Heath with his wife, Catherine, who was aged 35. The family detail given in the census returns shows that in 1851 just one son, Mark, aged three and born at Colney Heath, was present with his parents in the unnamed house next to the church. Two other occupants were servants. By 1861 the house is described as the Parsonage and Roche himself entered 'perpetual curate' as his occupation. Also present were Frederick Roche, a seven-year-old scholar, born at Colney Heath; a younger son, Ernest, aged four, also at school and born at Colney Heath; and two nieces, Elizabeth, aged

21, and Isabella, aged 18. Completing the household were Mary Ann Hubbard, a 23-year-old widow, who worked as a cook, and Jane Lambert, 16, a housemaid.

The census of 1871 – the year of Roche's death – was conducted in the spring when the head of the household's health was failing rapidly. The occupation column of the return gives the description Rector, while the house is shown as Vicarage. Another older son, Walter, aged 24, was present. He is described as a British subject, born in France. Mark Roche, by this time 20, worked at the GPO Savings Bank, while Frederick, 17, was a merchant's clerk. The presence of the three sons together indicate, perhaps, the seriousness of their father's illness.

During the spring and summer the household included Elizabeth Tibboth, a nurse, employed to care for the frail minister. Sarah Little, 22, from St Albans, was helping as cook. That William Roche was not officiating regularly at services is borne out by the fact that St Mark's had been assigned its first assistant curate. He was the Revd Edward M. Farley, aged 27, an unmarried priest, who lodged at the house of Mrs Louida Jackson, Colney Heath's grocer.

Young Ernest Roche, sadly, had died at the age of ten. His grave, marked simply with his name, age and date of death in 1867, is in the south-west corner of the churchyard, close to the boundary overlooking the garden of the house. There was another sad gathering in the churchyard, this time on 16 August 1871 following the death of Colney Heath's fourth incumbent. He is commemorated by a simple memorial stone; it describes William Roche as Rector of the parish.

PARSONAGE BY ANY OTHER NAME

Soon after the enactment of the New Rectories and Vicarages Act of 1865 a circular arrived at Colney Heath Parsonage from the Tithe Redemption Trust. Excitedly, St Mark's incumbent, William Roche, read that the trustees:

... beg to direct the attention of Incumbents of Perpetual Curacies to the fact that the Ecclesiastical Commissioners have now the power to constitute any such benefices a Rectory or Vicarage.

On the reverse was a hand-written note from the Trust secretary's office making clear that Colney Heath's benefice could be enhanced to either rectory or vicarage because the church endowment was in order with a qualifying tithe rent charge of £2588.17s.11d.

Mr Roche could not be directed more enthusiastically; he was keen to pursue the options. Before the end of September 1866 the Ecclesiastical Commissioners had authorised the apportionment of the rent-charge in lieu of tithes for the benefit of the present and future incumbents at Colney Heath. This order was eventually sealed on 8 August 1867 and then published, as required by statute, a week later in the *London Gazette*. Immediately Mr Roche took to styling himself 'Rector of Colney Heath'. It was all a bit premature.

True, he had published the necessary statement claiming rent-charges in lieu of tithes, and the application did not require the bishop's or patrons' consent. However, it did require payment of £1. 1s. 6d. for one further announcement in the Government official newspaper of the Commissioners' legal instrument and for a copy of

the newspaper to be lodged in the parish chest at Colney Heath. There is no evidence that the fee was ever paid. The only official notice preserved is the rent-charge apportionment; no copy of the *London Gazette* containing the final requisite notice was deposited in the chest.

Years later, after his retirement as vicar of Colney Heath, Laurence Bomford, the seventh incumbent, advised his successor in response to enquiries:

After August 1867 when the tithe redemption charge was granted to Colney Heath, the then incumbent (Mr Roche) always signed himself

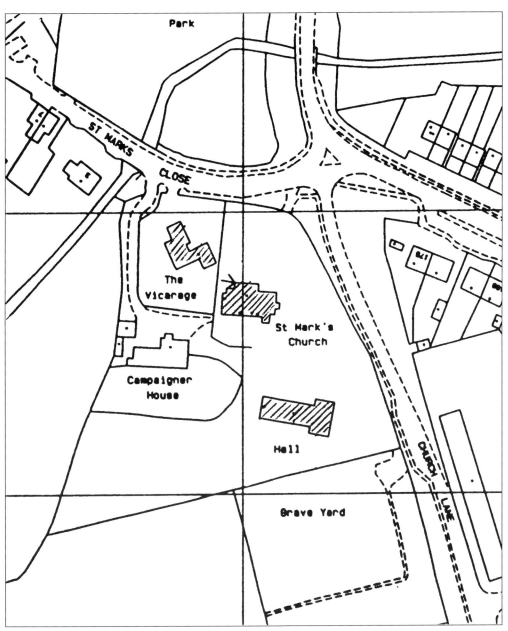

Today's relationship between church, vicarage and Christian centre. Here the mapmakers name the place of interments as 'grave yard' whereas the land immediately around the church, is churchyard, and the detached part, burial-ground.

Reproduced from the 2001 Ordnance Survey 1:2500 digital data map. © Crown copyright.

Rector. He could have done so legally by payment of a guinea which he never did. Harpenden paid a guinea and became a Rectory – it was previously a chapel of ease to Wheathampstead; Barnet paid a guinea and became a Rectory – it was previously a chapel of ease to East Barnet.

Bomford took issue with Edgar Jacob, third Bishop of St Albans (1903–20) who had suggested the legislation of such interest to William Roche had been rescinded 'because it brought such a rush of business that the authorities could not cope with it'. The former vicar argued:

The London Gazette *gives all the cases where the guinea was duly paid and shows that there was no such rush as our bishop imagines but, anyhow, a new Act was passed by which curates-in-charge could always be styled Vicar.*

Aware of the legalities or not, William Roche was content to style himself Rector of Colney Heath. He specified the description for his own headstone in the churchyard. No doubt, it was due to his aspirations, that on the 1:25 Ordnance Survey map of the time, Colney Heath's parsonage house was identified as Rectory: on some larger-scale OS maps it is still marked as such.

The schedule listing Colney Heath's rent-charges refers to tithes 'in the parish of St Peter in the Liberty of St Albans, in the County of Hertford.' Had the change William Roche set his heart upon come about, one consequence would have been that 'the repair of the chancel would not devolve on the incumbent of any newly constituted Rectory'. St Mark's, of course, did not claim to have a chancel. Imagine the chagrin therefore, when sometime later, the church-wardens were asked for a contribution from Colney Heath for the repair of the chancel at the mother church of St Peter's!

How well the ancient woodwork
Looks round the Rect'ry hall
Memorial of the good work
Of him who plann'd it all.

THE RAILWAY (1865–1968)

Thomas Carlyle (d.1881) believed the three great elements of modern civilisation were gunpowder, printing and the Protestant religion. However, the people of Colney Heath in Carlyle's time were profoundly affected by two further influences: the provision of education for all and railway transportation.

During more than two decades at Colney Heath, William Roche worked devotedly in the cause of education for the people. He was tireless in improving the reputation of the pioneer schoolroom in the High Street and in encouraging attendance there.

It was also in Roche's time that the railway came to the parish via the branch line connecting Hatfield with St Albans' Abbey Station. The line produced unimagined benefits in terms of communication, supplies, travel and new business once the local station opened. The twin influences of improved education and the new mode of transportation gave new dimension to life in Colney Heath.

The single-track GNR branch line opened in October 1865 towards the end of William Roche's fifteenth year in Colney Heath: it was to remain a working feature for 103 years. Roche was a great railway enthusiast and the opening of the line delighted him and the parishioners. While a station to serve Colney Heath had been planned on the route, it was not ready when the line opened. Originally the GNR had suggested a manure and coal siding only at Springfield with a small house for the clerk.

The siding idea did not go down well. If this was the Age of Machinery it was also a time of wider horizons. The people of Colney Heath called upon William Roche to petition the railway company for a proper passenger station: he took to this lobbying gladly and saw it result in a platform with a booking office and the usual buildings.

There was a delay in getting the station fully operational because of a hold-up in building the station house for the clerk. This resulted in Springfield station, half way along Smallford Lane, beginning as an unmanned halt. Eventually the stop was to become a much appreciated facility. Increased business contributed to the station being renamed Smallford for Colney Heath from 1 October 1879.

Seven incumbents of St Mark's made good use of the railway for themselves, their families and their guests. Some added the station's name and location, just half a mile distant, to their headed writing paper. Colney Heath people could take the train to St Albans for shopping trips; for years the return fare from Smallford was 4d. Stories abound about the railway's heyday.

*Smallford Station in September 1976, seven years after the track was taken up, post-Beeching–
a far cry from the day in 1889 when Lord Salisbury facilitated a special train to convey his
guest, the Shah of Persia, and his entourage, from Hatfield. They passed through on the way
to St Albans and thence via the Abbey station to Watford and on to Berkhamsted; all
without changing trains!* Photo: Brian Anderson.

**At Nast Hyde Halt on the
Hatfield–St Albans branch line,
lost in 1962 in the Beeching cuts.**
Photo: S.F. Page.

Smallford station in April 1988 looking towards Hatfield along the Alban Way footpath and cycle-track which replaced the railway permanent way.
Photo: Brian Anderson.

Shunting at Hill End, April 1960. Photo: M. Covey-Crump.

A pause to take on more water, then it's full steam ahead on Colney Heath's delightfully situated scale railway.

There is the account of a woman getting to the station just as the train began pulling out. Annoyed at missing it, she shouted to the footplate crew: 'You would have stopped if it had been the vicar!'

Around 60 years after the line's opening Smallford station witnessed the sudden death of a regular passenger who was a much-loved vicar of Colney Heath.

A headstone in the churchyard, west of the path to the porch, informs that John Kimp, who died in February 1900, aged 64, was for 21 years the station-master at Smallford. He started in 1879, the year of the station's name change. Serving before him were William Hayward and Edward Carver. John Kimp was followed first by Thomas North (1902–15) and then by George Dobson (1915–23). Nobody is listed between 1924 and 1927 and H. Lattimore (1928–32) was also in charge of Nast Hyde Halt. In 1933 both Smallford and Nast Hyde came under the responsibility of Hatfield's station-master.

Sadly, the railway stopped passenger services in September 1951 but freight traffic continued until the end of 1968, after which all the track was gradually taken up. Its bed gave way to the present walkway and cycle route. The arrival of the railway to serve Colney Heath was welcomed, and its departure, after more than 100 years service, mourned. Happily, the rail route is preserved as the Alban Way, a pleasant footpath and cycle-track linking St Albans and Hatfield.

Colney Heath's Little Railway

A dream came true for local youngsters (and their parents) in the shape of a ride-on steam model railway, when it was transferred to a site at Colney Heath waterworks grounds in the 1960s. It was good fortune for Colney Heath the day the model railway was relocated from its original site near Barnet, where the scale track had been developed by the North London Society of Model Engineers. The move was to make way for a water storage tower to be built on the original track-land at Arkley. The new site at Colney Heath proved idyllic and enabled the line to be better established and to run for about half a mile in a beautiful setting.

The gently curving looped track, served by its own station, Tyttenhanger for Colney Heath, with period lamps, seating and white wicket fencing, proved a summer haven for local families. While parents enjoyed the buffet bar, youngsters as well as the not-so-young, delighted in being hauled behind steaming replicas of classic locomotives. The mature landscape and the hard work of the railway enthusiasts fused together in perfect harmony for summer enjoyment with a difference. The ever-changing scene for the excited passengers, the intrigue of the working signal gantries and the whistle heralding the darkened steam-filled tunnel made visits pass all too quickly. The tell-tale drifting aroma of the model steam line outlived the real thing, fondly remembered as the Hatfield–St Albans GNR branch line that ran through the parish of Colney Heath.

The 1814 foundation stone of Colney Heath's pioneer school, as seen when set below the main window in the north wall of the High Street building.

EDUCATION FOR ALL

The School, Founded in 1814

The establishment of a school at Colney Heath, an extraordinary feat of pioneering education work 31 years before the church was built, came about as the result of direct influence of the clergy of St Peter's, St Albans. Early in the nineteenth century nobody thought in terms of government as a centralised body responsible for the welfare of the nation. Rather, in terms of employment, housing and social provision of the widest kind, the Church was the key source of godliness and practical concern in the lives of the people.

Of all 'good works', churchmen took education most to heart. If the Church thought education services needed improving or setting up, it provided church schools. Those schools emerged not so much from the institutional Church itself but from the input of inspired individuals. Britain has to be thankful that education in the nation state emerged from clerical origins.

Colney Heath schoolroom opened in 1814, as the result of concern for the children of the area expressed at St Peter's and particularly by the vicar at the time, the Revd Alfred William Roberts. It was not until William Roche's time in Colney Heath that the village school was put on a sound footing with the Charity Commission. This happened in 1869, on the application of Horatio Nelson Dudding who continued, energetically, to oversee important issues involving his daughter

church. Otherwise Dudding confined his rare visits for the purpose of conducting weddings or funerals where he had a particular connection.

Colney Heath Church School was already a registered charity with a reasonable endowment but there were no legally appointed trustees, a situation Dudding was determined to correct. He set about establishing a scheme for the future regulation of the school. William Roche signed the notice pasted to the door of St Mark's in the spring of 1869 detailing the proposals. There were no objections and so the incumbent and church-warden were appointed trustees to administer the school charity. The churchwarden referred to was Mark Tarry, then aged 37, a member of a local family with firm connections of service to St Mark's. His is the first name recorded as church-warden but he could not have been in office from the beginning, for he was born in 1832 and would have been too young. Nevertheless, he was most likely the first to be appointed to the office when he was older. Mark Tarry lived at Roestock, coming there from Princess Riseborough when he was about ten years old. The family worshipped at North Mymms before St Mark's was built.

The trust deed and other documents trace the control of the school, first from 1814, by St Peter's clergy and after 1845 by those of St Mark's. Through the years the progress of the school is mirrored, with extensions planned and various co-operative schemes between church and school

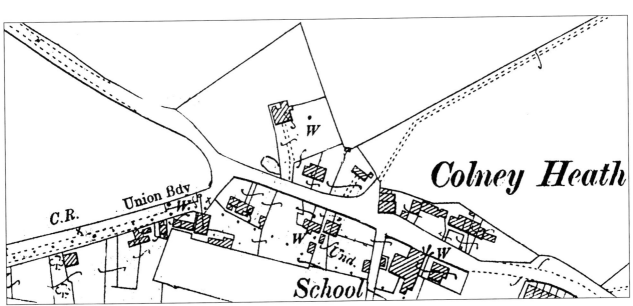

The site of the old school, on the south side of the High Street, is clearly marked on the map of 1898 together with the adjoining headteacher's house. Note the few properties on the south side of Park Lane and a cluster of homes, which no longer exist, to the right of the Crooked Billet. Four water wells served the population but Moonrakers, on the large site to the north, had its own well. Reproduced from the 1898 Ordnance Survey map.

announced. Only on one memorable occasion – to do with 'after school hours' use of church-provided furniture – was there anything approaching a rift between school managers and the church authorities. The lasting story from early times, through the days of the School Board to the County Council assuming complete responsibility, and up to the present, is one of cordial relationships.

Invariably, the vicar of Colney Heath has been appointed a school governor, often serving as chairman, as well as being welcomed to conduct school assemblies.

The Dudding trust deed spelled out everything in stark terms. It describes the original school site, taken out of the heathland, then belonging to the Earl of Essex, as measuring just 27 yards by 11; an adjoining piece of land, three poles by two poles was reserved for future expansion. Both pieces were to be:

... for ever appropriated and used for a school for the instruction of children and adults, or children

only, of the labouring, manufacturing, and other poorer classes in the district of St Mark, Colney Heath, and its vicinity, and for no other purpose.

The incumbent of Colney Heath was to have the 'superintendence of the religious and moral instruction of all the scholars attending the school.' He could continue to use the premises for a Sunday school. All other matters of control and management of the premises, funds, endowments, and also the appointment of the schoolmaster and schoolmistress and their assistants was to be vested in the incumbent, his curate if also nominated, and six others. These six had to be members of the Church of England, contribute at least 20s. a year to school funds and have a property interest in the area.

The first six managers to support William Roche to run the school were Mark Tarry of Colney Heath, William Smith of Hill End, Richard Clarke of Nast Hyde, the Revd H.N. Dudding, Henry Dymoke Green, of Oaklands, and John H. Rumball, of St Peter's Street, St Albans. Each was

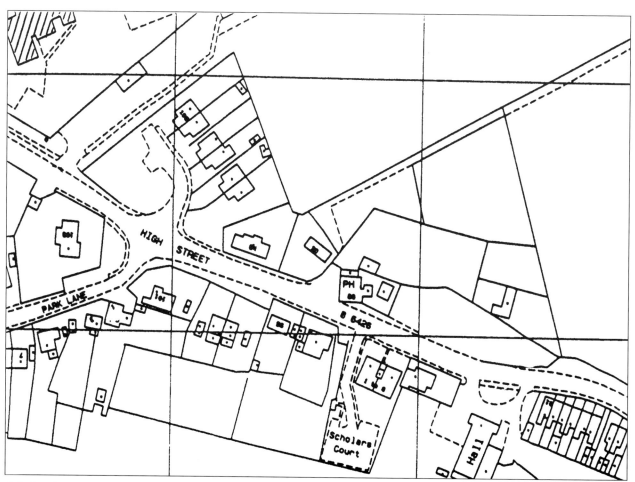

Scholars' Court occupies the old school site; the gap next to the school house gives entry to the 1938-built village hall. Six houses stand on the garden of the developed Moonrakers site and the pair of cottages next door were converted into one house. Reproduced from the 2001 Ordnance Survey 1:2500 digital data map. © Crown copyright.

Having your photograph taken in 1912 was a serious business. There was no smiling from these Colney Heath youngsters at the school's photo-call. Note the girls' smocks and the raked seating of the classroom.

required to sign in a book kept at the school the declaration: 'I...................., do solemnly and sincerely declare that I am a member of the Church of England.' A person who was not a member of the Church could not be appointed master or mistress of the school.

There was an elaborate procedure for resolving disputes. The incumbent or any committee member had recourse to the bishop if a dispute arose between them concerning: prayers used in school, the religious instruction of pupils and their regulation, the admission or exclusion of any book on religious grounds or matters affecting the dismissal of any teacher on account 'of his or her defective or unsound religious instruction of the children'. The bishop's decision was to be final. Other unresolved differences could be notified to the Lord President of the (Privy) Council and the bishop, who would each appoint an arbitrator, respectively one of HM Inspectors of Schools and a beneficed clergyman of the diocese (Colney Heath was still in Rochester Diocese at this time).

There was give and take. It was expressly provided that no child should be required to learn any catechism or other religious formulary or to attend any Sunday school or place of worship to which the parents had religious objection. All such matters were to be left to the 'free choice of such parents without the child thereby incurring any loss of the benefits or privileges of the school.'

The penultimate year of William Roche's incumbency saw Parliament pass the Elementary Education Act 1870. This gave opportunity, at the managers' request in July 1881, for administration of Colney Heath School to pass to the District School Board. The headmaster at this time, Nicholas Hambrook, embarked on keeping the school logbook, the requirement to do so having been ushered in as part of the Education Act ten years earlier. The school has a continuing set of logbooks from this period to the present day and they are a valuable record of progress over the years. Keeping logbooks became compulsory in schools receiving an annual grant as Colney Heath had started to do from the School Board. The regulations stated:

The logbook must be stoutly bound and contain not less than 500 ruled pages. The principal teacher must make at least once a week an entry which will specify ordinary progress, and other facts concerning the school or its teachers, such as dates of withdrawals, commencements of duty, cautions, illness, etc., which may require to be referred to at a future time, or may otherwise deserve to be recorded

The School Board had exclusive use of the premises every weekday from 8am until 5pm with parochial use outside the standard hours. This arrangement earned the school managers a peppercorn annual rent of 1s. The School Board also paid the rates, taxes, charges and other outgoings. This was good news for the managers who found the School Board also covered insurance and dealt with any repairs.

The Charity Commission had some awkward questions to ask in November 1892. It was found that income from the school's charitable funds was being paid by the managers – in good faith – for the benefit of certain local widows and old men. These parishioners had, at personal cost, been defraying the expenses of the Sunday school and night school as well as of the Sunday-evening services in the 'Iron Room'. This meeting-place had been erected in 1882 on copse land in the possession of the Gaussen family, to the south-east of the churchyard. The enquiring commissioners, while acknowledging the school's daily management remained with the perpetual curate of St Mark's, addressed their remarks to Colney Heath Rectory.

In November 1894, the St Albans surveyor and school manager, John Rumball, made a valuation of the premises. He found that:

... the old school has been very considerably added to and improved, now forming three classrooms fitted with galleries and woodblock floors, cloakrooms, etc.

The adjoining garden he remarked:

... has been enclosed by a new iron unclimbable fence and a schoolmaster's house built thereon in red brick with slated roof, containing six rooms and wash house, etc.

He gave the rental value as £18 a year. Mr Rumball also reported:

The property is all well and substantially built and

in good repair but being in a very poor locality and surrounded by small cottages is somewhat depricated (sic) in value and certainly not likely to be in anyway increased.

The valuation by Mr Rumball of the site at £75 and the buildings at £450 eventually led to discussions with the Charity Commission in 1895 for the transfer of the school itself to St Albans School Board.

In 1919, the St Albans watchmaker, F.G. Merkins, of London Road, fitted an unusual double-dial clock at the school. Mounted in the high-level front window, one face served the school itself while the other side could be seen by passers-by in the High Street. This useful clock continued to give good service right up to the day the building closed in 1969.

The school at Colney Heath flourished and was extended and improved considerably over the years. By the 1920s it had become Colney Heath County Council School No.175 with the designation of elementary school, taking pupils up to the age of 14. Its most celebrated headmaster was Mr Roland Richardson, appointed in 1923, who later went on to take charge of the much larger London Colney School. A former pupil-teacher from Christ Church School, Barnet, Roland Richardson, who became a JP, was prominent in Colney Heath affairs. Among many achievements, he was responsible for the campaign to build the village hall. He was instrumental in starting school cookery classes and these began in 1924 in church property – the old Iron Room – which had been repaired in 1897 with money remaining from that collected in the village for Queen Victoria's Diamond Jubilee celebrations. In 1903 the room was repaired again and extended to cope with the flourishing Sunday school transferred there from the day school building. This corrugated room had a lifespan of just over 70 years. Its successor in the

Inset: *Mr Roland Richardson was headmaster at Colney Heath School from 1923–1939. Before moving to London Colney School he became a prime mover in getting the site agreed for the village hall at Colney Heath.*

The teaching staff of Colney Heath School in the autumn term, 1969.
Standing (left to right): *Mrs Butler, Mrs Thomas, headmaster Mr J. Gibbon, and Mrs J. Willan;*
seated: *Elizabeth Lomax, Rosalind Stuchbery, Miss K.Waters, Mrs Sue Lilley and Mrs K. North.*

*Twentieth century youngsters
at Colney Heath School
celebrate a royal wedding,
1981.*

1950s seemed, initially at least, like a palace in comparison but this too was to run into difficulties. It did inherit a handsome Victorian wall dial clock with turned brass bezel, a mahogany case and a half-second pendulum: the clock was stolen when the post-Second World War hall was broken into in the mid 1970s.

Such is the chequered story of the formative years of the day school. Older than St Mark's itself, Colney Heath School has earned a creditable record of achievement; it has welcomed among its pupils children from the vicarage families over the years and it has been supported enthusiastically by the community and by the church. Above all, it enjoys a fine reputation for a happy environment.

The school's fortunes – from early days as a church-sponsored response for a deprived community, to becoming a modern county junior and infants school – have been steered by a succession of gifted headteachers. These include:

Mr W. Gray	in post in 1845
Nicholas Charles Hambrook	June 1881–September 1884
Alfred Robinson	September 1884–1885 (died November 1885)
Richard Payne	January–February 1886
Charles Fisher Pilbrow	March 1886–September 1894
Charles Richard Wimbury	September 1894–March 1898
Richard Cobden Jones	April 1898–December 1900
J.R. Markham	January 1901–July 1923
Roland Richardson	September 1923–October 1939
Albert Sergent	October 1939–December 1943
Walter Costain	January 1944–March 1944
Thomas Hodges	March 1944–July 1966
James Gibbon	September 1966–July 1982
Andrew Sawyer	(appointed September 1982)

Chapter Five

The Middle Years

TECHNOLOGICAL PROGRESS & TWO WORLD WARS

The years between 1880 and the beginning of 1933 were momentous times. A succession of five clergy served Colney Heath parish in a period when technology and new inventions raced each other: in homes people exchanged oil lamps for electricity and indulged in modern conveniences such as carpet sweepers and wind-up gramophones.

Colney Heath prospered and St Mark's Church became more comfortably furnished without extravagance. Some stained glass appeared in the windows, music developed when the organ was installed and the church tower was provided with a chiming clock. Electricity arrived proving a great boon but the two world wars numbed the village, which suffered a high death toll among its servicemen.

By 1900, creeping ivy was well established on the church walls.

The Revd George William Bailey
Vicar, November 1880–1898 (died 10 February)

Another Nelson Dudding nominee to the living, William Bailey, had served as curate and lecturer at St Peter's, St Albans the short time from 1878 until his induction at Colney Heath. In St Albans he had also been chaplain at the gaol. Before 1857 Bailey had been a minister in the Congregational Church.

William Bailey proved well-suited to Anglican parochial life. His wife, Mary, took an active part in church affairs during the 17-year ministry. This incumbent decided that he, too, was rector of Colney Heath, signing that way in the marriage register at the first wedding he conducted within a month of arrival. Six months later, in the census of 1881, the parish population was given as 749.

By 1882, Bailey completed the fund-raising for the first of three parish meeting places to grace roughly the same site between the original church-yard and the added burial-ground, south-east of the church. The first hall was the legendary Iron Room, a project dear to William Bailey and one to which he devoted a considerable amount of his own money in order that the growing Sunday school might be accommodated more comfortably. Messrs J.C. Humphreys, Roofing & Iron Building Works, of Albert Gate, Hyde Park, London erected the Iron Room for the princely sum of £148.6s.9d.

The new man paved the way for a lot of changes, but some of his alterations and additions did not always get recorded formally. A hand-written letter to Bailey, dated 14 September 1885, from St Albans' first bishop, Thomas Legh Claughton, states:

The improvements which you specify do not require a faculty – and you have my full permission to carry them out. Only I must point out to you that a Bishop's Permission is not the same thing as a faculty. If there were an aggrieved parishioner, he might sue you at law as having done such things without a faculty. But there seems no danger of this.

Bailey was assiduous in benefiting the people, when possible, as well as the church. In July 1881 he monitored a Charity Commission scheme regulating Sir Richard Coxe's charity of 1632 'for the maintenance of the church and its services and the poor of the (St Peter's) parish.' He got nothing for St Mark's, the daughter church, but managed to extricate an allowance of £16 a year for Colney Heath's poor.

He accomplished a number of necessary repairs to the church as well as the first major overhaul since it was built. This included the boarding of the ceiling, repair of pew platforms and improvements to the sanctuary including the introduction of carpeting. His crowning glory was the provision of the organ, erected in the gallery towards the end of 1887; it cost £100.

William Bailey was greatly mourned in February 1898 when he died in office at the age of 74. His wife, Mary Martin Bailey, died before him (on 10 October 1889) aged 63. Priest and wife are buried on the south side of the church in an area where a number of incumbents are laid to rest. The tombstone inscription to Bailey recites that he was 'for 17 years Rector of this parish'. He and his wife are also commemorated inside the church in the beautiful central lancet of the east window. Given in their memory, it depicts the Ascension.

Buried in the churchyard, close to their parents, are the Baileys' doctor sons. Henry James Bailey MB, CM, died aged 67 in 1932 on the same day in October that his mother had died; William Henry Bailey MD, died 25 April 1924, aged 68, and his wife, Kate Mary, died a month later (26 May 1924, aged 56). Kate Bailey is commemorated in the Good Shepherd window, in the south wall of the church overlooking the family burial-plot.

All the memorial stained glass was thoughtfully commissioned and is testimony to fine craftsmanship rather than the product, as was so often the case at this time, of pattern-book choices found repeated elsewhere in churches. The sanctuary window and the two in the south wall are the work of William Glasby, a talented artist, once employed by the leading church glaziers, James Powell and Sons, of Whitefriars, London as their chief stained glass painter.

Powell executed glazing commissions in churches throughout the country, including the fine stained-glass artistry produced by eminent Victorian designers such as Hardman, W. Hedgeland and William Wailes. A client of the company was the designer, Henry George Alexander Holliday (career 1863–1926). When he set up his own works' execution firm in Hampstead in 1891 he persuaded William Glasby to leave Powell and go into the new business with him. The partners went on to become stained-glass artists in their own right. The two Bailey memorial windows were dedicated in the interregnum of 1925–26. This was brought about by the death, also in office, of Colney Heath's eighth incumbent, the Revd J.B. Ost. He had prepared the dedicatory event in honour of the Baileys and had planned to conduct the service himself.

The central east window lancet depicting the Ascension *is a memorial to Colney Heath's sixth vicar, William Bailey, and his wife, Mary Martin Bailey.*

The Good Shepherd window (south wall) was given in memory of Kate Mary Bailey, William Bailey's daughter-in-law.

Photos: Brian Anderson

The Organ

While there is evidence that some music featured in services at St Mark's from early on – certainly there were singers in the gallery in the time of William Roche – it was not until William Bailey thought about organ accompaniment that the musical aspect of worship began on a new plane. The idea was clearly appreciated by the people in the pews who, by this time, were familiar with *Hymns Ancient and Modern*. They warmed to the thought of organ accompaniment, rather than the piano, for hymn singing and so it was that the psalms, as well as the canticles, were sung all through. It was only surprising, perhaps, that the change had come about through the enthusiasm of one who had begun in the ministry as a non-conformist preacher.

Preserved in the archives is a receipted bill, bearing a cancelled mauve Victorian penny stamp, from the organ builder, W.T. Hewitt, of Queen's Park, London. Dated 31 December 1887, it acknowledges 'the sum of £100 as agreed for building and erection of the organ in Colney Heath Church.' The documentary evidence is hardly necessary to date the organ accurately; clearly it was not envisaged as part of the original plan for the ordering of the church. Had it been so, even arriving years later, the instrument would never have been so inappropriately positioned, as it remains, with the casing immediately in front of the large west window

Set centrally in the gallery, the organ console and pipes obscure St Mark's west window.

above the gallery. Thus set, the instrument blocks out light. The magnified sun's rays through the glazing beat directly on to the pipes and casing. The organ was positioned where it is for convenience's sake; a shortage of space and difficulties in separating the console prevented the instrument being placed less vulnerably to avoid heat warping. It is likely that the original organ may have had one manual only plus pedals, or the swell section may not have been enclosed in a swell box. The organ, altered by Hewitt's in 1896 and added to in the time of the succeeding incumbency in 1911, had the following specification until 1988:

GREAT ORGAN		SWELL ORGAN	
Open Diapason	8	Open Diapason	8
Stopped Diapason	8	Lieblich Gedackt	8
Dulciana	8	Gemshorn	8
Principal	4	Cormo di Bassetto	4
Harmonic Fluter	4		

PEDALS

Swell to Great — (*Tracker action*)

Bourdon 16 — Great to Pedals — (*Mechanical stop action*)

Swell to Pedals

In 1988 the specification was upgraded to:

GREAT ORGAN		SWELL ORGAN	
Open Diapason	8	Open Diapason	8
Stopped Diapason	8	Lieblich Gedackt	8
Principal	4	Gemshorn	8
Harmonic Flute	4	Mixture	19/22
Fifteenth	2	Echo Trumpet	8

PEDALS

Swell to Great

Bourdon 16 — Great to Pedals

Swell to Pedals

The main alteration between 1911 and 1988, apart from repairs to the wooden pipes after splitting and repairs to the two keyboards, was the addition of an electric blower to replace the hand-pumping lever. The conversion to electricity was particularly welcome in the early days of W.E. Butland's incumbency. In an extremely busy life, Mr Butland's wife, Joan, and his son, Godfrey, had been prevailed upon to serve as the very last 'volunteers' to pump the organ manually.

After frequent siphoning and increasingly noisy and unreliable action, the decision was taken in 1988 that the organ should undergo major renovation and a partial rebuild. The London organ specialists, Page & Howard, carried out the work at a cost of £8000. The action was renewed using aluminium rod, the wind-chests cleaned and renovated, pipes regulated and fitted with tuning slides. Two ranks of pipes were removed and three new ones added with the swell box being enlarged to accommodate the additional mixture rank; the pedal board was replaced with a new straight and concave board. The new fifteenth and mixture ranks were scaled in accordance with the existing pipes and all the new ranks designed to enhance the original specification rather than alter the tonal quality of the organ.

The result of the rebuild is a fine instrument, well worthy of the pedigree inherited from its humbler predecessor; the purists are saved from the sound of the crematorium chapel, the organ is more responsive to the player and has an enhanced role in worship. Certainly, the instrument is better able to support the singing of congregations increasing in size. It seems fair to suggest however, that the church's pioneer organist back in 1887 would probably be unable to comprehend that the cost of the latest repairs could have purchased 80 organs at the asking price for the original instrument.

The Revd Laurence George Bomford
Vicar, April 1898–September 1918

Laurence Bomford was at Colney Heath for 20 years. Having researched the situation, he accepted the title and style, vicar, setting correct precedent for clergy succeeding him. Of greater concern to him was whether he would have the 'complete cure of souls' at Colney Heath because of some uncertainty about the status of the benefice. Bomford set about establishing the facts before ever setting foot in the village: he began a lengthy correspondence with the Church Commissioners, writing from the curate's house in Salisbury Road, Barnet during his final eight weeks on the staff of Christ Church. That town church was founded in the same year as St Mark's: its architect was the renowned George Gilbert Scott.

Bomford was born at Bembridge on the Isle of Wight. As a young man it was intended he should have a Services career, taking a commission in the Army, but he failed the medical examination. He turned instead to an interest in engineering and became the articled pupil of the well-known civil engineer of the time, Professor Pole. During his years of professional training Bomford developed his hobby as a landscape painter: this secondary interest took hold and he gave up engineering to become a full-time artist. In his new-found career Bomford studied under Mr Nathaniel Everitt Green, a Fellow of the Royal Astronomical Society, and he worked successfully as an artist for many years.

Laurence Bomford married Anne Green, the daughter of his tutor. Nathaniel Green was later to take a great interest in the church at Colney Heath. He started a fund to grace St Mark's with a turret clock, thus adding interest and a practical purpose to the charming but rather starved northwest tower. Nathaniel Green died in November 1899, aged 78. He was buried in the churchyard with the clock project unfinished. It was finally erected in 1901 as a memorial tribute to Green from his relatives, friends, pupils and Sunday school scholars. The fund attracted a £10 donation from Lord Grimthorpe, the restorer of St Albans Abbey and inspiration for the more famous clock, Big Ben, at the Palace of Westminster.

Always attracted to the church's ministry, Bomford abandoned his career as an artist in 1885 to enter Emmanuel College, Cambridge, where he gained second-class honours in theology and a Master's degree. He was ordained on leaving college and became curate at Barnwell, seat of the Gloucester royal dukedom, south of Oundle. His next move was to Trowbridge, Wiltshire, joining an old friend, Canon Henry Trotter, who was rector there. Henry Trotter left Wiltshire in 1894 to take the living at Christ Church, Barnet, then in the gift of his kinsfolk living a mile or so along the St Albans road at Dyrham Park. Bomford came to Barnet, too, staying as curate for four years.

He was not the only curate of Christ Church to move to the vicarage at Colney Heath and down the years there have been other connections between the churches. The links go back to the two churches' foundation just six months apart in 1845. The church at Barnet was established in thanks by Captain John Trotter of Dyrham Park following his conversion to Christianity in 1839.

As Christ Church, Barnet is within the prescribed radius for its incumbent to become a trustee of St Mark's, many vicars over the years responded to the patronage invitation. When it came to Henry Trotter's turn he was well positioned to influence filling the vacancy at Colney Heath in 1898. Laurence Bomford was 50 when inducted at St Mark's.

During his 20 years at Colney Heath, Bomford had the devoted support of his wife; her death in 1908 at the age of 59 was a bitter blow to the vicar, at what was the half-way point in his ministry. He continued a remarkable feat of keeping in touch with all the residents of the scattered parish. This cricket-loving vicar forged links with the youth of the district by starting a cricket club for the village. He played enthusiastically into old age for as long as his eyesight allowed.

Bomford also kept his hand in as a landscape painter and for many years he supported Hertfordshire Art Society. He loved walking on the common and once commented after leaving the village:

There is much of plant life, bird life and insect life to be found round Colney Heath; cuckoo and nightingales were plentiful – of the former we had one every year who sang a bit flat, while the latter had an entrancing repertoire. A horse was drowned one summer day at our gate while I was Vicar of Colney Heath, and one winter night a gamekeeper coming across the fields from supper at Tyttenhanger House wandered into a pond, where, two days later, he was found face downwards, dead, exhausted by his futile efforts to escape.

Bomford nurtured the school, relishing the implications of partnership afforded by the Education Act of 1902 which phased out school boards. He improved the Iron Room for the benefit of the ever-expanding Sunday school and proved to be the right man for the parish in the face of the heart-ache of the First World War.

In the year the war ended Bomford's health entirely broke down and he resigned the living. He returned to Barnet for a few years before moving back to St Albans. He returned briefly to Colney Heath in October of 1923 and in May 1925 to conduct the baptisms of two nephews. The former vicar lived in York Road until his death in the last week of July 1926. He was 78. Laurence Bomford was buried alongside his wife, next to the grave of her parents, immediately to the south of the church. Interment followed a simple service at which there were no hymns or music. The late vicar's brother, the Revd Trevor Bomford, gave the address.

A sadly ironic situation arose over the memorial plaque proposed for Laurence Bomford and his wife. The final version, as submitted by the parish and eventually granted faculty approval, may be seen on the south wall of the church. The Chancellor of the Diocese had earlier refused to allow the family motto to appear on the tablet because it was in Latin; the refusal is revealed in correspondence written after the already prepared alabaster tablet was cut and lettered. There were further objections to the order of some of the lines on the memorial and to the use of an abbreviation. Most strenuously opposed was the proposed description of the vicar's wife as a 'minister of the Word'. The authorities insisted on instructing changes conditional to faculty consent: the reference to Anne, in the line below the tribute to the vicar, was the permitted final revision – 'his wife and fellow worker'. The rejected version is preserved because, no doubt to save expense, the reverse face of the original lettered stone was used for the amended tribute. The rejected words remain, unseen, dowelled into the wall. It is also worth mentioning that the ordination of women was neither an issue nor even a talking point at the time. Since the problem with the Bomford plaque no further memorials to St Mark's clergy have appeared in the church.

Right: A fund for the church turret clock, to benefit the people of Colney Heath, was launched by Nathaniel Green. Erected in 1901, the project became a memorial to Green, following his death in November 1899.

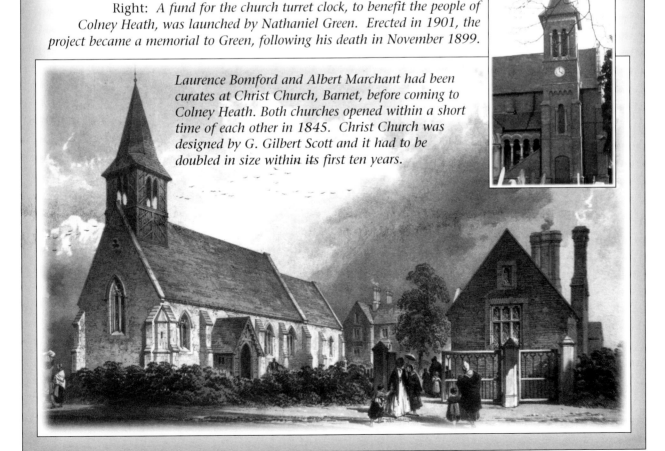

Laurence Bomford and Albert Marchant had been curates at Christ Church, Barnet, before coming to Colney Heath. Both churches opened within a short time of each other in 1845. Christ Church was designed by G. Gilbert Scott and it had to be doubled in size within its first ten years.

Storm clouds over Colney Heath common.
Photo: Weston Marchant.

*Attended by the Diocesan Registrar, the Bishop of St Albans, the Rt Revd Michael Furse,
signs the Deed of Consecration of the burial-ground extension, opened off Church Lane in 1923.
Robed is Colney Heath's incumbent, the Revd John Browne Ost. Behind the bishop and
registrar is cathedral verger, John Wilkins, and to the right are St Mark's churchwardens,
H.J. Selborne Boome and R.C. Hart Dyke.*

The Revd John Browne Ost

Vicar, December 1918–1925 (died 28 November)

Pictured Left: *The Revd John Browne Ost pictured with the fourth Bishop of St Albans, Michael Furse, on the right.*

John Browne Ost arrived in Colney Heath shortly after the end of the First World War. Immediately he was involved in plans for the village to mark the peace in the following summer. Two years on the church saw its most solemn occasion – the unveiling of the memorial to the 36 young men of the village who never returned to celebrate the end of the war to end all wars.

The new vicar had devoted much of his life to missionary work. Born in the west of Ireland in 1851, he prepared for his vocation first by studying in 1876 at the Church Missionary College, Islington. He was ordained deacon in 1879 and went to China that year to serve with the Church Missionary Society at Shaouhing. Following his priesting in 1881 he spent another 30 years working in China: for his last three years there (1906–09) he was examining chaplain to the Bishop of Chekiang. On his return to England in 1909, he became a member of the C.M.S deputation staff. From 1913 until his appointment in Colney Heath Mr Ost lived at St Albans while working as the society's organising secretary for Ely and St Albans dioceses.

John Browne Ost was an affable, courteous and hospitable incumbent during his Colney Heath ministry which lasted just seven years and ended abruptly with his tragic death at Smallford. The vicar had been the inspiration for raising a large sum of money for the church repair fund. He improved further the Iron Room and acquired for the parish the freehold of the land on which it stood. He negotiated for the new burial-ground, made possible by the gift of land by Mr Charles Morris, motor engineer, of Highfield Hall; and he worked tirelessly to enhance the endowment fund.

Ost took a keen interest in public administration; he nurtured close links between the church and the local civil authorities, which have remained close and cordial over the years. Parishioners at St Mark's had taken active parts in organisations concerned with civic and public service, but John Browne Ost was the first incumbent of Colney Heath to serve as a member of an elected body: for three of his seven years he sat on St Peter's Rural Council – representing, prior to St Albans Rural District Council, both Colney Heath and London Colney. The villages shared one parish council until the formation, in 1947, of Colney Heath Parish Council.

Near the end of his episcopacy, Bishop Edgar Jacob had been welcomed to St Mark's churchyard by Mr Ost for the dedication of the remaining small and hitherto unused portion of land kept for interments. This was carefully plotted in rows A–H with 19 burial spaces in each. However, Mr Ost had an eye to future needs, hence negotiating for ownership of the copse abutting the original churchyard to allow access through it to the land given by Charles Morris. The extension burial-ground was intended to serve the parish to the end of the twentieth century. The site was consecrated in 1923 by Bishop Michael Furse (1920–45).

Two years later, on 28 November 1925, Colney Heath was stunned at the tragic suddenness of the death of Mr Ost at the age of 74. It was a Saturday morning and he had been on the platform at Smallford Station awaiting the train to Hatfield where he was to see churchwarden, Mr W.H. Sherriff. The vicar was suddenly taken ill, and, despite attention from station staff, died before medical aid could be given. After a post mortem examination an inquest was conducted by the St Albans coroner, Mr T. Ottaway. His verdict was that Colney Heath's vicar had died from natural causes following heart failure brought about by valvular disease.

Many clergy from neighbouring parishes and farther afield attended the funeral at Colney Heath the following Thursday and the church was filled. Bishop Hodges, who had known Mr Ost for over 50 years, gave an address. The interment took place on the south side of the church. The vicar's widow, Mrs Mary Jane Ost, died in February 1946 aged 87. She is buried in the family grave which also commemorates Frances Amy Ost, a daughter (died 2 January 1952) and Kathleen, second daughter (died 18 November 1963) – they both lived locally. The eldest daughter married and two more became teachers and moved away from Colney Heath. There was also a son, Mr H.T. Ost.

During the interregnum before the appointment of Albert Marchant, services at Colney Heath were conducted by the Revd Trevor Bomford, brother of the parish's former vicar.

CELEBRATING PEACE

The peace celebrations at Colney Heath on 19 July 1919 were lavish by any standard and entirely funded by public donations. Bands, parades, entertainment, sport and tea for everyone brought the population out on to the streets and common. Every item of expenditure was scrupulously accounted for with stamped receipts filed away.

Well documented, also, was the carefully organised campaign to honour Colney Heath's war dead with a suitable memorial. The initial idea was for a great granite cross, ten feet high, set in the churchyard, on a raised stepped base some five feet square. The St Albans stonemason, Edwin Seymour, worked out how the names could be shown in leaded lettering on each of three designs. The finished project was expected to cost £100 but the plan proceeded no further; all three designs were rejected.

Public interest in the memorial was intense. It was to be the first time such monuments would be allowed to break from the convention that, apart from dates and places, only the names of battles and field marshals could be incised. Now there was consent for local memorials to be personalised with the names of the nation's young men lost to their communities.

Finally, it was agreed that Colney Heath's tribute should be placed in a prominent position inside the church. A central space on the east wall to the north side of the apse was chosen for the veined alabaster portrait tablet. Measuring 48" x 27", the memorial stone, fashioned by Gawthorpe & Sons, London, artificers in brass, iron and marble and warrant holders to King George V, was fitted at the cost of £84.

Colney Heath's population at the start of the First World War was 1500. Over 100 men from the village volunteered to join the Colours and of these 36 laid down their lives. The inscription begins with the words:

In ever grateful memory of the following officers and men of this parish who fell in the Great War 1914–1918. Greater love hath no man than this, that a man lay down his life for his friends.

Stoker	W.	HARLAND	HM *TBD *North Star*	Pte	A.	SIMPKINS	East Kents
L/Cpl.	A.	PAYNE	1st Beds Regt	Pte	J.	MUNDY	1st Essex Regt
Pte	G.	DOCKREE	1st Beds Regt	Pte	J.E.	MATTHEWS	Grenadier Guards
Pte	E.	ALLEN	1st Beds Regt	QM Sgt	A.	RISEBERO	1st Herts Regt
Pte	W.	LEONARD	1st Beds Regt	Pte	H.	KENT	1st Herts Regt
Pte	A.	CHILDS	1st Beds Regt	Pte	W.J.	WINCH	King's Royal Rifles
					Corps		
Sgt Maj.	W.	REYNOLDS	2nd Beds Regt	L/Cpl	E.	REYNOLDS	9th Lancers
Pte	W.	ALLEN	2nd Beds Regt	Pte	Jos	McNAIR	15th Lancs Fusiliers
Pte	C.	MANSEL	2nd Beds Regt	Sgt	W.	SCOTT	Machine-gun Corps
Pte	Jos	RAY	4th Beds Regt	Pte	A.	SMITH	7th Manchester Regt
Pte	W.	RISEBERO	4th Beds Regt	Pte	A.	MILES	2n Middlesex Regt
L/Cpl	E.	PAYNE	6th Beds Regt	Pte	W.	COOK	2n Middlesex Regt
L/Cpl	F.	COOK	7th Beds Regt	Sgt	S.	MANSELL	4th Middlesex Regt
L/Cpl	E. J.	MARDELL	7th Beds Regt	Pte	A.	ALLEN	12th Middlesex Regt
Pte	G.	BRETT	7th Beds Regt	L/Cpl	D.L.	GRAY	Royal Garrison Artillery
Pte	F.	RAYNER	7th Beds Regt	Pte	T.W.	PINK	Royal Welch Fusiliers
Pte	C.	HART	8th Beds Regt	Pte	H.L.	GRAY	Seaforth Highlanders
2nd Lieut. Ernest GRAHAM			12th Border Regt	Pte	J.	BRETT	Tank Corps
* Torpedo Boat Destroyer							

Left: *Fine detailing of the north porch and outer stone stairway at St Mark's. The design is based on the Norman stairway at the King's School, Canterbury.*

Below: *The veined alabaster memorial, listing the names of Colney Heath's 36 young men who perished in the hostilities of the First World War, was placed on the east wall of the church and to the north of the sanctuary. The memorial was unveiled just before Christmas, 1920.*

The unveiling and dedication of the memorial took place in a packed church a few days before Christmas 1920. A huge parade through the village was led by St Albans Ex-Servicemen's Band while in church Miss Gertrude Ost, the most musical of the vicar's five daughters, played the organ. Mr Ost and the Archdeacon of St Albans, the Ven. the Hon. Kenneth Gibbs, officiated. Lord Queensborough unveiled the memorial. The proceedings were reported in the *Herts Advertiser*. The newspaper quoted from the sermon where the Archdeacon suggested that as long as the church stood in Colney Heath the names on the memorial would testify to the duty done for the village in the strain and darkness of war.

Following the poignant 1920 service, the large congregation went out into St Mark's church-yard to the spot where the only village casualty of the First World War to be brought home is laid in the shadow of his parish church. The name of Private W.J. Winch, King's Royal Rifle Corps, had been read from the memorial: then parishioners gathered round in the cold air as an honour guard of his comrades fired three rifle volleys over the grave in salute. The grave, once marked by a simple wooden cross, is no longer identifiable.

The Revd Albert Marchant
Vicar, May 1926–December 1932

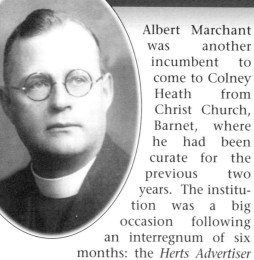

Albert Marchant was another incumbent to come to Colney Heath from Christ Church, Barnet, where he had been curate for the previous two years. The institution was a big occasion following an interregnum of six months: the *Herts Advertiser* reported it fully and included a photograph of the new vicar, a Licentiate in Theology, plus one of the procession of clergy passing between an honour guard of Scouts, Girl Guides and Brownies. A few days before the service, the vicar's wife, Mary, had given birth to their son, Ronald Marchant. He was baptised at St Mark's by Albert Marchant's former boss, the Revd Samuel Roberts, for 40 years vicar at Christ Church. Ronald Marchant followed his father into the parochial ministry. He was not the only 'son of the manse' at Colney Heath to become ordained.

Albert Marchant packed a lot into his six and a half years' stay in the village. Having just had the two Bailey windows installed, the church was to benefit further from a number of 'best oak' furnishings to transform what was still a very basic interior. On Sunday, 30 June 1929 a new pulpit was dedicated by assistant bishop Lander. There was also a new clergy desk and sanctuary rail, within which there was a matching oak credence table. A shelf was placed below the war memorial to accommodate flower holders. The sanctuary was completed with a Persian rug, set on new blue felt designed to harmonise with the reredos curtain. The curtain covered completely the words of the Apostles' Creed and the Ten Commandments painted on the wall of the apse – thus negating the Victorian statute requiring the tenets of faith to be displayed prominently in all churches.

The new furnishings had cost £130.10s., the most expensive item being the pulpit at £70. The supplier was the Faith Craft Studio of Victoria Street, St Albans who rather than giving a discount, donated a fall for the lectern.

This concession meant a new oak hymn board could be afforded and a 'really well made one' came to another two guineas.

Albert Marchant's tenure continued along well-ordered lines. It was he who suggested a new challenge for congregational singing – *Hymns Ancient and Modern Revised* – and, delighted with a choice of 700 hymns, promptly organised practise hymn-singing sessions. 'If we rehearse these hymns together then you will know exactly what the organist is going to do, and the result will give satisfaction', he claimed. No doubt, the organist, too, got a fair appreciation of the singers' abilities.

In May 1927 everyone was still a little unfamiliar with the role of the newly-introduced parochial church councils. Mr Marchant's PCC had no difficulty in passing a resolution opposing the introduction of the proposed 'new' prayer book, which came to be known as the 1928 book after the year of its eventual publication. The revision had been approved by the General Assembly of the Church of England but had been rejected by Parliament. After Marchant's time and despite the earlier PCC ruling, the revised prayer book did appear in the pews at St Mark's.

Albert Marchant resigned the living in December 1932 to take charge of the parish of Christ Church, Felling-on-Tyne, near Gateshead. Later, he took appointments in parishes in his favoured North Yorkshire. His last appointment was at Bletsoe, Bedfordshire, before retiring, in 1960, to live near his son, Ronald, who was then an incumbent in Suffolk. Mr Marchant, who was survived by his wife, died in May 1970.

COLNEY HEATH'S NEW VICAR INDUCTED.

The Revd. Albert Marchant at his institution at Colney Heath.

CHURCH FURNISHINGS

It was during Albert Marchant's incumbency that the first determined effort was made to soften the rather austere internal ordering of St Mark's. There was a move towards better quality furnishings and improved decoration with a view to making the church a more welcoming place. If St Mark's was perceived as a 'preaching barn', then the preaching continued but in a much improved and more comfortable environment.

By far the greatest number of faculties permitting changes in the church were granted in Albert Marchant's time. The majority were sought as the result of generous gifts and bequests and there was a rush in his time for reservation of grave spaces in the new burial-ground.

Sometimes gifts presented problems. There was a dilemma when a well-intentioned lady from the congregation offered a new communion table for the church. The table in situ was really quite adequate for the purpose and it had been presented in 1925 by the Marchioness of Salisbury (Lady Cicely Alice Gore), wife of the 4th marquess. Lady Salisbury's gift to the church had been gratefully received; it replaced the original table bearing incised consecration crosses and which the Bishop of London had laid hands upon at the consecration of 1845.

Now there was a third table. It was to be of oak, beautifully carved and designed to match furnishings given in 1929. It was agreed the Cecils could not be upset over the issue, especially when it was remembered that Lord Salisbury had made a most generous donation towards the cost of the organ. The situation was delicate. Marchant instructed the PCC secretary, Miss Louisa Edwards, to send a carefully-phrased letter to Hatfield House. It succeeded both in its mission and in being just short of unctuous.

Lady Salisbury was advised about the re-ordering scheme at St Mark's, into which, it was said, the Holy Table on offer to the church would suit admirably. Had her Ladyship any wishes for the disposal of the table she had graciously presented? The letter begged the issue slightly by suggesting that if the faculty sought for the replacement table was granted, then the Hatfield gift might go to a new mission church within the diocese. Lady Salisbury acquiesced. The faculty for the new table – still in position – was granted on 30 September 1930 and St Luke's Church, The Camp, St Albans received the Salisbury table. Everyone was happy, especially Mrs Christabel Rose Burton, whose generous gift had resulted in testing diplomacy all round.

Occasionally, the wishes of donors and the church were frustrated – as in the case of the Bomford memorial – when applications for faculty were not straightforward. Approval could never be a foregone conclusion, as was proved by the case surrounding the dramatic stained-glass window by William Glasby, depicting St Michael, above the vestry door. All was approved apart from the detail of the background sky colour. The window donor, Mrs Elizabeth Wilson East, had a dark blue sky rejected because – it transpired – the specification would restrict daylight into the church. The diocesan registrar insisted on plain glass quarries and the window, with these changes, was approved in April 1931. Mrs East had given the window in memory of her husband, Joshua Harman East, of Highfield Hall, who had died on 10 April 1882, aged 52, and of their son, Edmund James East (who died 29 September 1929, aged 48). The dedication states simply: 'This window is given by the wife and mother.' The window was installed and unveiled 18 months after Edmund's death. Two months later, Elizabeth East died, aged 83.

Albert Marchant was the first to propose major re-ordering for the church. For much of the work he secured a draft works specification from an architect friend back at Christ Church, Barnet, Mr W. Charles Weymouth. He advised, in November 1930, a plan more radical than

Inset: *The skill of the accomplished stained-glass painter and glazing designer, William Glasby, is seen in the dramatic depiction of St Michael installed in 1931 in the window above St Mark's vestry.*

improving simply the look of the pine panelling on the north and south walls. He was for shortening the pews and inserting aisles between them and the walls, then panelling with oak from dado level to the floor. At this time the choir occupied the gallery. Mr Weymouth told Marchant:

I entirely sympathise with your desire to bring the choir down to the main floor and I am preparing a sketch to show how it can best be done. It is almost essential to enlarge the church somehow (a) to provide vestries and (b) to accommodate the choir without encroaching upon the seating.

Mr Weymouth, who lived in Barnet until the mid-1960s when he died in his nineties, commented on the 'many good points' about St Mark's. It was, he said:

... a church built in a style which it is almost impossible to make look well in modern materials and to meet requirement, but yours has a quite exceptional character which should be maintained. With a little care I believe suitable additions can be made and the present building greatly improved without excessive cost.

He was ahead of his time. He further stated:

It will be said that the burials which have been made so close to the church preclude enlargement. I know the difficulty, but I cannot believe that the living representatives of the dead will offer persistent objection when they know the need,

neither do I think it likely that the Chancellor would support them to the point of refusing a faculty.

Mr Weymouth had perceived the enlargement situation precisely but he under-estimated the feelings of those families with kin that had been buried, regrettably, too close to the church walls. Over the years since, development plans have been frustrated because of relatives' interests in burials near the vestry and at the west end, as the result of unmarked interments close to the pathway. The west end had to wait until 1986 for radical change.

Agreeing to a new west door at a raised outer level on the turn of comparatively narrow steps was, perhaps, not the most inspiring faculty recommendation by the Diocesan Advisory Committee. A more gracious entrance, at ground level, leading to a narthex, might have served better than the elevated arrangement at the head of raked seating, descending in a style more than a little reminiscent of Odeon. The west-end faults, however, are more than redeemed by the sanctuary and vestigal chancel re-ordering, which has created a delightful, practical and welcoming spaciousness.

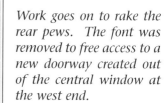

Work goes on to rake the rear pews. The font was removed to free access to a new doorway created out of the central window at the west end.

The west end central entrance.

The church's restoration
In eighteen-eighty-three
Has left for contemplation
Not what there used to be.

The Revd George Weston Byers-Jones
Vicar, January 1933–July 1952

A colourful personality, the tenth incumbent at Colney Heath experienced a testing 19 years. He served between the wars, during the Second World War and into the post-war era. He worked hard sustaining the parish in the difficult years from 1939–1945, and comforted war widows and children made fatherless. George Weston Byers-Jones witnessed symptoms of the national malady of the time – the abrupt drift away from religion in the immediate post-war years. There were, however, Churchillian 'bright sunlit uplands' too. It was to Mr Byers-Jones that fell the job of organising the modest celebrations marking the centenary of the church at Colney Heath, one month after the war ended.

The PCC had drawn up a profile of the person they wanted at the vicarage. Preference was expressed for a married curate. Short of specifying someone with the virtues of the Archangel Gabriel, the PCC secretary, Mr G. Gordon Cooper, of Marlboro House, Colney Heath Lane, wrote to the bishop with the advice:

He should be in the prime of life. Members feel that church interests would greatly suffer if an elderly man should be appointed to the vacancy, the age mentioned being not over 45; spiritually minded, evangelical with broad outlook.

Since 1927 the then plain George W.B. Jones had been curate at St Cuthbert with Christ Church, Bedford where he lived in Waterloo Road. He had journeyed from much farther afield and reached Colney Heath in possession of the Archbishop of Canterbury's permission to officiate under the Colonial Clergy Act. He had spent the early years of his ministry (1913–22)

in a variety of appointments in Canada: in East Toronto, Alberta, Prince Edward Island and Nova Scotia. He returned to Britain in 1923 to take a curacy for three years at St Jude's Church, Brixton.

He was licensed at St Albans by Bishop Michael Furse. Colney Heath's new man had complicated things slightly before his arrival in the parish by suddenly choosing to change his name. For years his surname had been simply Jones until he added to it – by deed poll – his third Christian name, Byers. The paperwork for the induction at St Mark's had been prepared ahead of the name-change and the vicar-to-be was told by the diocesan registrar: 'I am unable to use the hyphen since it is not possible to legally adopt one Christian name as part of a surname.' The registrar's advice to the vicar was to call himself George Weston Byers Byers-Jones. This drew the prompt protest: 'I do not want to add to the length of my name' and from that moment he used the deed poll name.

Byers-Jones had first sight of St Mark's by the light of Blanchard oil lamps. Now electricity was available and a faculty was granted in February 1934 for an electric lighting scheme, the cost of which was borne by the congregation and friends of Mr Selborne Boome. For a change it was a gift in appreciation of the living; he had just completed 14 years service as churchwarden. The small plaque to the right of the vestry door records the installation of electricity into the church in March 1934.

Later the same year there was alarm when the church suffered a dry rot attack in the deal panelling in the north-east corner, affecting the dado decoration given only two years earlier as a memorial to Mrs A.F. Harrison. The £120 bill for remedial works was a bitter blow: it put on ice the building fund for a new church hall to replace the decrepit Iron Room. Nevertheless, the fund had an encouraging £250 balance. Early in 1938 a cross of beaten brass, 27″ tall, for the communion table, was given in memory of Mr Charles Barker: the faculty also gave permission to dispose of the existing cross and six matching candlesticks.

The autumn found Mr Byers-Jones in hospital. He had a successful operation and recovered in a London nursing home. The vicar's wife took the helm running church organisations including the usual September fête. This featured a physical training display by the Church Lads' Brigade under Lieut. Christopher Tarry and CSM L. Gulliver.

Life in Colney Heath continued in a half-muffled peal sort of way for the six agonising years of the Second World War. Another 22 young men from the village, mainly single men but some married with young wives and families, lost their lives in hostilities. It was to the vicar that people turned in sorrow and looked for comfort in cheerless times before the invention of the welfare state. The village itself did not escape enemy action: it was plagued particularly by the new ballistic terror, the dreaded flying bomb. Over-shooting London, as they did frequently, one just missed the vicarage and church, and exploded in a field nearby. The church roof and some windows were damaged in the blast but services went on uninterrupted.

Canon Glossop of St Albans Cathedral (second left) meets with retired churchwarden, Mr J.C. Simmons, and his successors, Mr R.C. Hart Dyke (left) and Mr H.J. Selborne Boome.

There were two dramatic war-time incidents in the village. A great tragedy was the loss, in October 1943, of a Lancaster bomber which plunged from the skies to a spot on the Warren, killing all seven crew members. A more sinister descent from the skies – little known about at the time – centred on the stealthy arrival of Karel Richard Richter, a 28-year-old Obersturmfuhrer, whose parachute dropped him in a field to the south-west of the common. Code-breakers at Bletchley Park knew of the spy's impending arrival in Britain as he had been entrapped in an MI5 counter-espionage operation. This was aided by a degree of co-operative civilian vigilance typical of the local ingenuity employed in rural areas to ferret out and intercept enemy agents.

Richter, a German national, born a Sudeten Czech in Kraslice, descended early in the morning of 14 May 1941 in a spot west of the Colne and about halfway between Parkgate Corner and Tyttenhanger. Immediately he hid his parachute in a thicket not far from the river and

Karel Richard Richter

Richter tells of his 'get away' route the previous night.

After enemy spy, Richter, was arrested he revealed where he had hidden his parachute.

Dressed in overcoat and trilby, Richter waits, unconcerned, while security personnel examine his parachute.

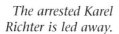

The arrested Karel Richter is led away.

Photography by Harold Dearden.

concealed himself for the rest of the day. That evening he broke through the hedge, emerging from the Caledon estate on to the North Orbital roadside verge and headed westward. Richter's undoing was in failing to be able to give coherent directions to a lorry driver who had lost his way. Puzzled by the pedestrian's strange response, the driver pulled away, and, at London Colney, by good fortune spotted a policeman. It did not take long for the country bobby to pursue investigations by heading his bicycle in the direction of Colney Heath in search of Richter.

Constable Alec Scott, who shared duties in London Colney and Colney Heath with PC Tom Day, eventually caught up with the German agent in a telephone box at the Barnet/St Albans crossroads. Challenged, Richter produced an authentic Alien's Registration Card in the name of 'Fred Snyder'. However, there was less than an hour to go before the alien was supposed to heed the curfew rules and be at the registered place shown on the card. That was a London address and it would have been impossible to get there in time. Constable Scott, however, had ample time to size up his interviewee. He was certainly suspicious of the tall, thin, red-headed figure, by then clad in bulging topcoat and wearing a trilby hat. Scott telephoned the police station at Fleetville for a patrol car and some backup. Searched on arrival at Fleetville, 'Snyder' was found in possession of a Swedish passport in the name of Karel Richter. He was held to await the arrival of a military escort the next morning. Back in the police Wolseley, the young lieutenant storm trooper was driven to Hatfield police station. There he was exhaustively interviewed by a seven-strong delegation from MI5's German espionage unit from Latchmore House on Ham Common, where Richter was later detained.

Richter co-operated with his interviewers, readily agreeing to show them where he had landed the previous day near the Colne. The MI5 team returned to the spot with Richter. He showed them where he had hidden the parachute and they took possession of the spy's field wireless, a loaded automatic weapon, his Czech passport and his money – 1000 US dollars and £300 sterling. During this reconstruction of events, Dr Harold Dearden, MI5's expert on interrogation techniques, took a series of remarkable photographs, including those reproduced in this book. However, Richter's help proved to be limited. He resisted every threat and inducement to collaborate with the 'Doublecross' operation aimed at feeding the enemy misleading intelligence.

Local people who got to know of the events were unaware of the organised entrapment situation; Richter had been destined to travel from rural Hertfordshire to London. His arrest caused the cancellation of that MI5 initiative. Great speculation arose over what might have been the purpose of Richter's mission, given the vulnerability of war-time operations in the immediate area of his landing. Had Tyttenhanger House been targeted because of its connections with Field Marshal Alexander of Tunis? That was unlikely; the war leader (whose earldom came in 1952) was busy elsewhere and he was last remembered at the park ten years earlier for a short stay at the mansion on his honeymoon. Richter had landed within easy reach of Hatfield airfield and the works of the de Havilland Aircraft Company. There were secret establishments, too, at Butterwick Farm, Smallford and off Sandpit Lane. However, the drop was more on target for the temporary airfield near the Bell Lane/St Albans road junction and for Salisbury Hall, the nearby moated manor house requisitioned as a suitable decoy place for the design and manufacture of Britain's Mosquito aircraft. The prototype, W4050, heralded a grand total of 7781 planes and was the most successful of aircraft employed in the wartime battle of the skies. In the spring of 1941, only days before Richter's arrival, a Mark II Mosquito, entirely designed and assembled at Salisbury Hall, was flown by Geoffrey de Havilland from the sloping parkland at the back of the house to land successfully at Hatfield.

Almost certainly Richter's mission was to provide information on Hatfield aerodrome or on Salisbury Hall. Minus local signposts and without maps he failed at the task.

Richter's silence at the Tyttenhanger 'discovery' and his refusal to join 'Doublecross' effectively signed his death warrant as an enemy agent caught in the field; he was one of 16 spies executed in Britain during the Second World War. Arraigned at the Old Bailey for a trial in camera before Mr Justice Tucker in the autumn of 1941, he was found guilty and sentenced to death on 21 October. As Richter was a civilian and not a member of the German armed forces, he evaded military custody and trial by court martial. This also meant he avoided the death sentence being carried out at the Tower of London by firing squad. Instead he was committed to Wandsworth Prison. On 10 December, shortly before being led to the scaffold trapdoor, Richter put up a sudden desperate struggle with Britain's hangman, Albert Pierrepoint, and his two assistants. The behaviour amazed the MI5 officers present, who knew of the parachutist's quiet surrender following his arrival on a bright May morning in a peaceful meadow close to Colney Heath common.

*The moated manor house, Salisbury Hall, where the Mosquito,
Britain's wartime prototype aircraft, was designed and built.*

*The Mark II Mosquito was flown by Geoffrey de Havilland from the parkland
at the back of Salisbury Hall. It landed successfully at Hatfield airfield.*

The entrance to Salisbury Hall across the moat. Nell Gwynne was housed in a cottage in the grounds. Winston Churchill's mother once owned the house and a later occupant was Nigel Gresley, the locomotive engineer.

The Byers-Joneses relished a break in the austerity of the immediate post-war period afforded by St Mark's low-key centenary celebrations in June 1945. The *Herts Advertiser* commented: 'the charming village church stands as a memorial to what can be accomplished when the will to advance God's work is there.' Clergy from neighbouring churches crowded into the Friday evening special service at which the preacher was the Archdeacon of St Albans, the Ven. C.T.T. Wood. He brought a message from the new Bishop to St Albans, the Rt Revd Philip Loyd (1945–50), who commended all Christians to seize the opportunity to put God back into His rightful place in the national life, thus enabling the peace to be rebuilt on the surest foundation.

The very smallest members of Mrs Byers-Jones' Sunday school, dressed in white, sang a specially-composed hymn. The youngsters were a roll-call of Colney Heath family names down the years: Thelma Mansfield, Violet Reynolds, Ruth Arnold, Sylvia Nash, Jennifer Day, Esther Scott, Glenda Littleworth, Anne George, June Lloyd, Tommy Day, Bobbie Day and Michael Swain.

After the service there was entertainment on the vicarage lawn by the older Sunday schoolchildren, plus a display by the Church Lads' Brigade. Refreshments followed in the ailing Iron Room, its funds benefiting from the centenary services' collections.

At the principal Sunday service, the preacher was the St Albans assistant bishop, Bernard Oliver Heywood. He was diocesan bishop of Southwell (1926–28) before translation to Ely. The vicar had hoped the centenary festival would encourage the building of a new meeting hall worthy of the church and parish in replacement of that described as being 'in an advanced state of decay'.

Spirits had been lifted at a time when life was made difficult by shortages and rationing. Communications were speeded up when the vicarage went on the telephone. The original three-digit number – Colney Heath 227 – outlasted mechanisation when dialling facilities were added to the switchgear housed in the tiny exchange at the High Street crossroads. The cosiness ended early in the 1970s when all Colney Heath subscribers were given four-figure numbers – later increased to six – when they were added to the Bowmans Green exchange.

The well-remembered Mr Byers-Jones retired as Colney Heath's vicar in 1952; he died at the end of 1957.

Colney Heath roads were less congested in the 1970s.

Great Nast Hyde was the home of Colney Heath churchwarden, Reginald C. Hart Dyke.

Popefield Farmhouse, flanked here by cow shed, granary and implement shed, was the home for 40 years of John Thomas Patience, farmer, overseer and churchwarden at Colney Heath for 14 years. He died in 1903, survived by his wife, Eliza, who died in 1923.

Local Houses

The manor house at Tyttenhanger Green, better known as Highfield Hall, in common with larger estate houses in the district – Great Nast Hyde, Tyttenhanger, Yeomans, and North Mymms – was regarded as a residence for the gentry. These houses and their occupants gave 'tone' to Colney Heath as the community developed and lost the abrasiveness of its wilderness image.

A nearer but less important house on the fringe of the parish, Popefield, is a charming oak-framed sixteenth-century farmhouse of three storeys. Recorded as the occupant in 1876 is John Thomas Patience, farmer and overseer, a great supporter of Colney Heath Church for 40 years, 14 of them as churchwarden. He died in May 1903, aged 64, and his widow, Eliza Ann, survived him until June 1923. From Eliza's death until 1938 the occupants of Popefield were Marriott and Watkins, corporate farmers. The de Havilland Aircraft Company then acquired the property on the perimeter of the airfield close to the Hatfield Road. The original granary, cow shed and implement shed, were, like the ancient house, sympathetically restored by British Aerospace in 1981.

After the last war the pioneer aircraft company was incorporated into the British Aircraft Corporation. It was during this time that Tim Rice, the theatre lyricist who went on to work in partnership with Andrew Lloyd Webber, lived at Popefield as a child with his parents and brothers, Jo and Andy. Their father was a senior executive at Hatfield aerodrome. The boys attended St Albans School before going on to Lancing College. In the longer school holidays, notably at Easter, remembers the Revd W.E. Butland (1958–80), the family attended St Mark's Church, sitting near to the Popefield memorial plaque of the Patiences. Could it be that the religious instruction young Tim received on his visits to St Mark's sowed the seeds that later inspired him to co-write the successful musical Joseph and the Amazing Technicolour Dreamcoat?

STRANGE LEGACY

At Tyttenhanger Green, the East family were occupiers for some years of Highfield Hall. Like previous owners, including the renowned Charles Morris, they had become generous benefactors to the community and to the church. As well as the family window in the church, St Mark's inherited an elaborate churchyard monument, erected in memory of Joshua Harman East. The double-width burial-plot, within iron horizontal rails, in the south-west corner of the churchyard, cannot be missed. The memorial base of three tiers of dressed stone designed to take inscriptions on four sides, is surmounted by a rugged rock on top of which is hewn a large cross entwined with a remarkably detailed chain and anchor.

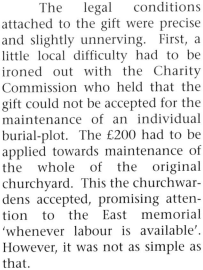

During the Second World War, bomb damage at a London solicitor's office – causing important documents to be lost – added to the intriguing story about the chain and anchor monument at Colney Heath. A letter from the solicitors arrived at the vicarage in July 1942 on behalf of the executors of the Will of Ida Florence East, the spinster daughter of Joshua and his wife Elizabeth. Ida East had died three years before, on 28 August 1939, but the bomb damage had held up grant of probate. The letter delighted George Weston Byers-Jones who found the church on the receiving end of a legacy of £200 for the upkeep of the East memorial.

The legal conditions attached to the gift were precise and slightly unnerving. First, a little local difficulty had to be ironed out with the Charity Commission who held that the gift could not be accepted for the maintenance of an individual burial-plot. The £200 had to be applied towards maintenance of the whole of the original churchyard. This the churchwardens accepted, promising attention to the East memorial 'whenever labour is available'. However, it was not as simple as that.

Miss East had specified that the family tomb be kept in good order and repaired, as a condition of the gift. Her executors pleaded the legal conditions be met even though the churchyard as

Inset: *The huge chain and anchor memorial stone to Joshua Harman East and other members of the family whose home was Highfield Hall.*

a whole was to benefit. 'Good order' meant that the lettering on the monument was to be kept legible and re-cut from time to time if necessary. Additionally, the stonework was to be washed down once every three months.

It seemed the churchwardens were to earn the money the hard way and there was worse to come. If the monument was not kept in good repair, or if the lettering could not be read and was not re-cut as instructed, or if the stonework went unwashed for six months, then the £200 would be lost. The capital and its accrued interest would be transferred from St Mark's and go instead as a gift for London's St Bartholomew's Hospital. The Easts had strong connections with the hospital and what was to become its rural annex.

Churchwarden Harry John Selborne Boome, stockbroker, of Ellenbrooke Lane, and crafter of diplomatic correspondence on behalf of St Mark's proceeded skillfully. The church would act in the spirit of the Will and with regard to the money having to benefit the whole churchyard. St Bart's was keen to test matters. The Clerk to the Governors, no less, wrote to the vicar and church-wardens on Christmas Eve, 1942, in a Dickensian style reminiscent of a scene from *A Christmas Carol*. The letter stated that the gift remained valid for the upkeep of the churchyard so long as the vicar and churchwardens kept the East memorial in good condition. Also rehearsed fully was the provision for the transfer of the fund to the hospital. The letter ended:

In view of the foregoing, I shall be glad if you will let me know the date upon which the said monument was last washed for the purpose of our records.

Churchwarden Selborne Boome enjoyed his Christmas and New Year festivities unfazed. In January he replied that the monument had been washed down 'on or about' the beginning of November and that the spirit in which the legacy had been given would be honoured. The final recorded salvo, in 1943, stated that the Governors of St Bart's would consider it their duty, from time to time, to enquire as to 'whether the gift over in favour of the hospital has taken effect'.

Members of the East family were living at Highfield Hall before the outbreak of the Second World War in 1939. There was clearly a close affinity between the family and St Bartholomew's. This was cemented in the early days of the war, when, amid heightened fears that central London

Hill End Station in 1959. Coming from Hatfield, the engine and brake van head for the Salvation Army depot siding.
Photo: M. Covey Crump.

was about to be bombed, most of the patients and nursing staff of St Bart's were evacuated to a new temporary home within less than a mile of Highfield Hall. Over 300 nurses from the London hospital found themselves in Colney Heath parish at Hill End, which was a designated psychiatric hospital. By 1940 St Bart's had established more than 1100 general beds at Hill End Hospital. Within two years the greatest concentration of patients was in the military wing.

Freight deliveries to the hospital via the railway siding serving the hospital increased dramatically.

As a salutary reminder to future Colney Heath churchwardens, a framed copy of the East memorial 'rules' appeared in the vestry at St Mark's. Several holders of the office, including the writer, can testify to first washing the monument, then red-oxiding and painting with black enamel the railings round the last resting place of Joshua Harman East of Highfield Hall.

SECOND WORLD WAR MEMORIAL

Still in Mr Byers-Jones' time, the memorial to Colney Heath's men who gave their lives in the Second World War was not put in place until shortly before the Remembrance Day service of November 1948. On Sunday, 3 October, the new tablet was dedicated by the fifth Bishop of St Albans, Philip Loyd.

The memorial, exactly matching in style and dimensions that of the 1914–18 tablet, was unveiled by Lt T.W. Gould VC, RNVR. The First World War tablet had been repositioned so that the two memorials, bearing a total of 58 names, could be spaced centrally on the east wall, to the north side of the sanctuary.

The service, arranged by George Weston Byers-Jones, included – at the moment of unveiling – a fanfare by buglers of the lst Battalion Hertfordshire Regiment TA. Mr F. White, of Tyttenhanger Green Baptist Chapel, read the lesson. Then the 22 names on the new memorial were read out: the sad duty of doing this fell to the man who had taught so many of them as pupils at Colney Heath School, their sorrowing headmaster, Mr Roland Richardson.

Beneath the inscription:
In ever grateful memory of those in this Parish who gave their lives in the Second World War 1939–1945, appear the names of the fallen:

Commando	R.E. Baldock	Royal Marine Commandos
Private	A.G. Beach	Somerset Light Infantry
L/Cpl	H. Beale	The Buffs
Able Seaman	R.R. Bramwell	Royal Navy
Private	J.J. Bush	Beds & Herts Regiment
Bombardier	B.G. Chamberlain	Royal Artillery
Sgt Gunner	J.R. Day	Royal Air Force
Trooper	M.P. Ellis	Reconnaissance Corps
Lt Col	S.M.E. Fairman	General List
Stoker	S.D. Hard	Royal Navy
Private	A.D. Harris	Northamptonshire Regiment
S/Sgt	C.H. Hart	Royal Army Service Corps
Private	F.G. Heffer	South Staffordshire Regiment
Private	J. Heffer	Beds & Herts Regiment
CPO	J.F. McEune	Royal Navy
Sgt Pilot	H.G.J. Middleton	Royal Air Force
Cpl	L.J. Pollard	Queen's Own Royal West Kent Regiment
Private	C. Potter	Cambridgeshire Regiment
Driver	A.T. Simpkins	Royal Artillery
Cpl	D.A. Sturman	Royal Corps of Signals
Private	H. Wigfield	Gordon Highlanders
Sgt	J.M. Wood	Royal Marines

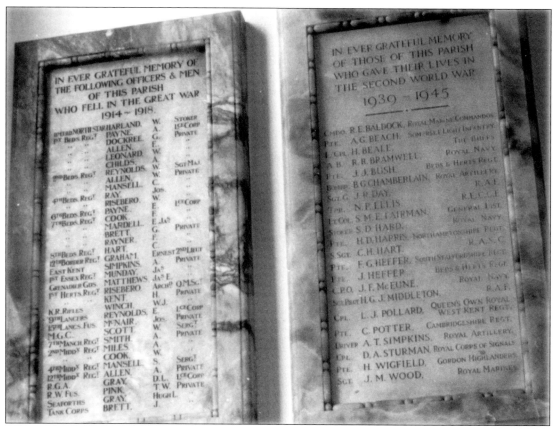

The mural alabaster memorials to the fallen of two world wars;
58 names of servicemen from Colney Heath families are recorded.

A THIRD WAR MEMORIAL

It was not until 50 years later, in 1995, the one hundred and fiftieth anniversary year of the church, that a memorial was put in place to accommodate the names of any Service personnel killed in conflicts since the end of the Second World War. In only one of those years was there no military loss by British forces.

By Remembrancetide 1995 (at which point D.R. Veness was vicar, 1980–98) the post-1945 memorial had been added beneath the two alabaster ones. Petitioned for by Colney Heath Parish Council, who are statutorily responsible for additions to war memorials in the parish, the simple brass plaque, bearing just the one name, reads:

In ever grateful memory of those of this Parish
who gave their lives while serving their
country in the Armed Forces.

Malaya 1948–1960
Trooper P.J. Totman IV Queen's Own Hussars

In August 1949, Peter John Totman, a former pupil of Colney Heath School, was killed during the second year of the Malaysian crisis. He was one of 340 to perish in the conflict and he died in the arms of his comrade and close friend, L/Cpl Bernard Bruton, who returned to Colney Heath after his National Service, and, years later, became churchwarden at St Mark's.

When you go home, tell them of us and say:
"For your tomorrow we gave our today."

Chapter Six

Prologue to Modern Times

THREE INCUMBENCIES FROM 1954

The clergy whose ministries occupy most of the last third of Colney Heath's 150-year history as a parish have demonstrated pivotal roles in the life of the village and the church. Each emerged to leadership at the right time, ministering to the community and sustaining the church in times of joy and adversity.

The three holders of the living from 1954 to the one hundred and fiftieth anniversary of the parish in 1995 complete 13 incumbencies since 1845. They have presented a contrast of personalities but each will be remembered. In common with clerical predecessors, their combined contributions to parochial life will only truly be appreciated in the fullness of time. They have endeavoured to teach and encourage by word and precept. Their ministries, that helped prepare local people to cross confidently into a new millennium, are indeed worthy of reflection.

The Revd Ross McPherson Heard
Vicar, May 1954–February 1958

The amiable presence of the new man at the vicarage was warmly welcomed in the village. St Mark's had just emerged from its longest time without an incumbent – two years. This, following on the heels of the slow climb out of post-war doldrums, had far from benefited the community, the church or the parish.

Ross McPherson Heard was very tall; literally he stood head and shoulders above many of his parishioners. There was another tall, striding personality in the affairs of Colney Heath at this time. He had a passion for cross-country running and jogged around Verulamium Park lake before breakfast: he was the sixth Bishop of St Albans, Michael Gresford-Jones (1950–1970) who had been obliged to impose the long wait for Colney Heath's new vicar. His presentation suspension order delaying the trustees nominating a candidate had been made pending an examination of the future of the church and benefice.

The examination was thorough, taking into account more than simply the effects of general post-war malaise which had affected many parishes. Attendance at St Mark's had slumped after the war and, consequently, the parish had dire financial problems. A small and loyal congregation supported the church and gave generously but the burden was falling on too few.

In the months without a vicar things went from bad to worse. One likely option – the least undesirable – was that the benefice might be combined with that of St Paul's (built 1910) in Hatfield Road, St Albans. The view got about that St Mark's might never have another vicar of its own; worse still, was the thought that the church might be made pastorally redundant

Inset: *Colney Heath's 11th vicar, the Revd Ross McPherson Heard, with his wife, Valerie.*

and effectively closed, or at best, used as a mortuary chapel. All such rumours appalled the regular congregation who tackled the serious situation with new resolve. The generosity of the congregation in self-help, giving and greatly improving contributions to the diocesan quota was duly recognised.

When he arrived on 18 May 1954, the welcome reserved for Ross McPherson Heard, as the new incumbent, his wife, Valerie, and two small daughters, bordered on the ecstatic. The devotion to the people shown by the personable new vicar meant bridges were soon built again. He was able to bring the church to the parish and the people back to worship, maintaining a faithful ministry and approachable style throughout his stay of four years.

Ross McPherson Heard completed his training for the ministry at Clifton Theological College, Bristol. He was priested in 1942. Like his predecessor, he was a Dominions man and came to Colney Heath from New Zealand. There he had looked after three churches in Amuri, North Canterbury in New Zealand's South island. Bishop Gresford-Jones offered him quite a contrast in the job to be done at St Mark's.

Life at the church began its recovery, very slowly, out of the negativism of the early 1950s. Things were not easy and the post-war deprivations pressed hard. An early priority was to do something about a meeting-place for the parish and its organisations: all the wringing of hands had to end in favour of action. The result was that the vicar rolled up his shirtsleeves to lead the men and boys of the parish in putting up a build-it-yourself hall.

The new building was far from being an architectural masterpiece: it could never have been so considering the restrictions of the time. Building materials were still hard to come by. Indeed, certain components were impossible to get and some raw materials were either restricted or completely unobtainable. Thus the hall turned out rather reminiscent of much of the post-war housing it imitated in style – the ubiquitous stop-gap prefab. The self-assembly sectional building, with a flat roof, was, however, an enormous improvement on what had existed before. The new hall was an age away from the years of iron rooms. With an entrance lobby, main hall, small meeting room, plus a small kitchen, it was far better than most

had imagined possible in the circumstances.

The new facility was something genuinely appreciated until it outlived its usefulness. The trouble was, enforced years of usefulness proved to be far longer than the temporary planning consent granted relative to a modest life expectancy. That it survived so long was some testimony to the basic ruggedness of the building. The hall went on long after its 'sell by' date but not without considerable patching up in its final years and bailing out in bad weather.

Outside, in the summer months, garden parties resumed at the vicarage, with guest openers such as the Earl of Verulam. One very memorable visitor, resplendent in crushed pink with feathers, Mrs Hugh McCorquodale – better known as the prolific romantic novelist, Barbara Cartland – was to interest herself in Colney Heath's gypsy community settled on the common.

New life in the parish resulted in the re-establishment of a full choir under the direction of Mr G. Allen with Gerald Millington as organist. Church music and singing improved dramatically and the competent choir became robed.

The McPherson Heard family, like vicarage families before them, had been obliged to augment the heating in the house to keep winter chills at bay. The laborious job of stoking the old coke-fired boiler beneath the west end of the church finally came to an end.

Ross McPherson Heard continued his ministry at Colney Heath until February 1958. For his health's sake he sought a living in the West Country; he became rector at Hatch Beauchamp with Beercrocombe, and from 1962 until his retirement in 1976, combined the appointment with that of the benefice of West Hatch in the diocese of Bath and Wells. He then moved to Cambridge in 1978. At the time of St Mark's one hundred and fiftieth anniversary, Colney Heath's affectionately remembered former vicar, then aged 84, and Mrs McPherson Heard were enjoying quiet retirement in one of the city's attractive tree-lined avenues not far from the retired eighth Bishop of St Albans, the Rt Revd John Taylor, KCVO (1980–1995). Ross McPherson Heard died in January 1998, aged 87.

Inset: *A young and vivacious Barbara Cartland opened one of the summer garden parties held in the vicarage grounds at Colney Heath.*

Right up to the time the choir came down from the gallery to occupy shorter, front pews that turned to face north and south, the interior of St Mark's kept a familiar, traditional appearance. Note the glass pendant light fittings.

The Revd William Edwin Butland

Priest-in-Charge/Vicar, 24 June 1958–31 August 1980

W.E. or 'Joe' Butland, as he became affectionately known to parishioners and bishops alike, was not inducted until he had served a first year at Colney Heath. Before his arrival there had been a three-month suspension of presentation to the living. The reason for delaying the formal appointment and effectively denying the usual parsonage freehold and other rights was linked to the impending deanery boundary changes. As vicar, even of a few days, the new man would be consulted about boundary changes but as curate-in-charge they could be put in place without reference.

When he did arrive, parishioners were charmed by Mr Butland's soft, melodious tones, indelible in the speech of a true West-Country man; it was a joy to hear his sermons. He was born in Bristol and brought up in Devon, going straight from school into HM Dockyard, Devonport, as an apprentice electrical fitter.

His first abiding love was railways, especially his beloved Great Western. This interest took him into the divisional civil engineer's drawing office at Plymouth. Later he transferred to the chief engineer's office at the line's 'cathedral', Paddington. From 1930 to 1948 Mr Butland's GWR – God's Wonderful Railway – as later sermons would have it, took him on working assignments to Gloucester, Newport and Plymouth before he finally qualified as senior surveyor and draughtsman.

The track change came in 1948 when he entered the shortly-to-close St Andrew's Theological College, Pampisford, Cambridge. He transferred to the London College of Divinity, which because of war damage at St John's, Highbury, was housed temporarily at Ford Manor, in Lingfield, Surrey. The principal at that time was the Revd Dr F. Donald Coggan, later to become the one hundred and first Archbishop of Canterbury.

William Butland was over 40 when he was ordained at Michaelmas 1951; he served his title at London's Kentish Town parish church and the following year was ordained priest at St

The vicar and Mrs Butland with their children, Godfrey, Rosemary and Hilary, meet with the Bishop of Hertford, the Rt Revd A.J. Trillo.

At the 125th anniversary celebrations of St Marks, the vicar was presented with a framed enlargement of the architect's design for the north-west elevation. On the left are churchwardens Richard Ostler and Bernard Bruton.

Paul's Cathedral. In 1954 he moved to Chorley Wood, Herts, in semi-sole charge of St Andrew's, then a daughter church of Christ Church.

Taking into account his curacy year at Colney Heath, he served for just under a seventh of the parish's first 150 years – a total of 22 years and two months, edging him only just into the lead as the longest-staying occupant of Colney Heath vicarage. There was a lot to do in the parish, and the church itself was at a post-war watershed. Colney Heath was not going to remain a rural backwater, yet manpower and resources to meet needs were limited.

Mr Butland had at his side, his wife Joan, who in a quiet, modest and charmingly winning way, did much to help tip the delicate balance in favour of knitting the parish together. Together the Butlands were a formidable force that achieved much progress during challenging times at Colney Heath; things were pretty rustic when they first arrived. The elderly gardener, Mr Hill, was still using a scythe for cutting in both churchyards: eventually he was persuaded to try a new motor-powered mower acquired by the vicar, having encouraged the civil Parish Council to contribute towards the cost. The Parish Council remained supportive, contributing also to the churchyards' upkeep and towards repairing the church clock.

A little local difficulty maintaining good public relations came via the Chancellor of the Diocese issuing new, mandatory regulations governing churchyards. New rules banned kerbs and ledger slabs, controlled the dimensions of headstones, advised on epitaphs, and in particular, specified natural, indigenous and sacrificial stone for memorials rather than white marble and foreign imports. The logic was supposed to be perfectly understandable: mourners wishing to have memorials crafted in polished coloured granite, with unsuitable words, carved excesses, photographs of loved ones and edge-to-edge purple 'bath salts' chippings had the option to arrange burials in municipally-controlled cemeteries. Logical it may have been, but it represented a pastoral minefield for the new vicar soon after his arrival.

The Butlands shared a great burden for the youth of Colney Heath. They proved themselves adept in relating to the young, a skill no doubt fostered partly by their three children, Godfrey, Rosemary (both later to be ordained) and Hilary. All three attended Colney Heath School. The vicar and his wife were soon plunged into youth club work, developing the Sunday school and initiating a Pathfinder group. Activities at this time were shared between the spartan hall near the church and the Roestock Room, a former outpost inherited from North Mymms parish following boundary changes.

Within a year of their arrival, the vicar and Mrs Butland helped re-kindle the uniformed organisations, with the intention of them becoming church organisations. [See Chapter Seven for more information on clubs and organisations.]

Innovations seemed endless at this time. The parish population of a few hundred was suddenly heading for 3500 and there was a lot of new housing. There was the beginning of renewed interest in the church by young families moving to the village; all augured well. One highly successful development was the holiday club which began as meetings for youngsters on August afternoons. At first they met at the Roestock Room and later transferred to the school. The club was soon re-launched as an annual venture lasting a week. Volunteers from the church trained themselves to run the well-supported event which proved popular among children, helpers and parents.

The old tin tabernacle at Roestock was the venue for special study meetings held each Lent. The first house groups began at Firwood Avenue and at Moonrakers. These were followed by parish days and weekends, which became regular annual events.

The Butlands were the first vicarage family to enjoy the new home provided by the diocesan parsonages board. Memories soon faded of their first move into the original vicarage, which in 1958 still had no mains drainage. Excess rain soon filled the cesspool and caused great problems. With three children to be kept away from such hazards, the diocese bowed to pressure and eventually connected the house to mains drainage.

The church choir of young people and adults expanded. When George Allen left, Herbert Harris, the organist, took over the direction. He was followed by Bob Roome, whose son, Simon, and another young treble, Richard Lilley – both unaware of each other's intentions – found themselves one Saturday morning competing for one of an unspecified number of choristerships at St Albans Cathedral. Stephen Darlington, a gifted young musician, newly arrived from Canterbury as Master of the Music at the Abbey, was holding the first ever competitive public voice trials. There were eight young and nervous boys hoping to become cathedral choristers and don the red cassocks. In the event, Darlington chose the two nine-year-olds from Colney Heath: it was a decision reflecting justifiable credit on the musical tradition and training at St Mark's. Richard Lilley went on to become a Woollam Scholar in the cathedral choir and then head chorister.

Mr Tony Bralant was the next organist and Heather Bennett became musical director. The appointments led to some inspiring organ and piano accompaniment, the introduction of the

The notice on the door advising 'No collections are taken at this church', often featured in the questionnaires for weekend car-rally competitors.

Two young members of Colney Heath church choir, Simon Roome and Richard Lilley, won places as choristers at St Albans Cathedral after competing in an open voice trials competition.

singing group, the Ichthians, and altogether, a wider variety of music, plus a more informal style for the developing family service.

The church had come a long way in a short time, though old habits died hard. When Mrs Butland was in the village one day, a woman pressed sixpence into her hand, whispering, 'it's for the vicar'. The donation was intended for a stipend fund to assist a then smaller congregation in supporting the ministry directly!

On their arrival the Butlands were confronted with an extraordinary form of heating in the church. An industrial blower was in use to propel – through a grille at the west end – hot air from a heater fuelled by propane gas. This amazing piece of farming technology might have been satisfactory for crop drying or to keep hens roosting happily, but it did not sit easily with Transitional Norman style, c.1845, or its congregation 113 years later. Out went the wafted air machine and in came neat, efficient, electric tubular heaters fitted under the pews.

Despite the difficulties and temptation for the vicarage family always to be doing too much, the real purpose of St Mark's forged quietly ahead. Coffee mornings, pram services, prayer and Bible groups, informal services and much more came about in the Butland years. Greater numbers were attracted to an interest in the church and its mission. A turnaround was beginning; gradually fewer people considered themselves to be flying buttresses – supporters from the outside.

Joe Butland played a large part in the campaign to make crossing what was known as the North Orbital Road – which had split the parish in two – a safer business. Originally there were two separate and dangerous crossroads just west of the church. The High Street went over to Sleapshyde Lane and the more direct route, in front of the church, led to Colney Heath Lane. The redundant short spur, after road changes, needed a name and the Butlands suggested St Mark's Close. As a thank you for pressing for the footbridge over the trunk road and a variety of roundabouts before the eventual 'long-about' appeared, the old lane might equally have rejoiced as Butland Way.

The vicar sprang his retirement decision on to a surprised congregation. They packed the village hall for an evening in honour of the vicarage family in a 'This is Your Life' tribute concocted by churchwardens, Cliff Harvey and Bryan Lilley. Between that warm-hearted occasion and the Butlands' final day at the end of August 1980, the vicar succeeded in doing something he had found little time for in all his 22 years at Colney Heath. Accompanied by his family, he went for a walk across the common. It was, he testified, as pleasant an experience as his predecessor 60 years before – Laurence Bomford – had vouched.

From Colney Heath Mr and Mrs Butland went to the little village of Wootton in Bedfordshire where they began helping at the church and, not surprisingly, leading very busy lives. With Joe Butland in his nineties, he and Mrs Butland finally embraced proper retirement in 2001 when they moved to a village near Rugby, close to the home of their younger daughter and her husband.

Mr and Mrs Butland in the garden of their home at Wootton, Bedfordshire.

A mare with foal on the common in the spring of 1971.

The Revd David Roger Veness
Vicar, 1 December 1980–March 1998 (including the one hundred and fiftieth anniversary, December 1995)

Above: *The 13th vicar of Colney Heath with the Bishop of St Albans, the Rt Revd John B. Taylor.*

It fell to David Veness, the thirteenth incumbent, in December 1995, to steer the celebrations marking the one hundred and fiftieth anniversary of St Mark's foundation. It was also the fifteenth anniversary of the vicar's arrival in the parish. A series of special events brought parish and village together. The anniversary service was very much a shared occasion, one of acknowledgement of the people that had contributed to the life of the church and parish down the years. The Revd Clive Calver, of the Evangelical Alliance, preached at the packed service, which was relayed by video-link to an overflow congregation. Then everyone adjourned to Nicholas Breakspeare School in Colney Heath Lane for lunch and more celebrations. That *Past is Prologue* never rang more true.

Towards the end of 1980 the churchwardens had coped with an interregnum of just three months. Even so there was relief when Bishop John Taylor telephoned with news that a young curate from Birmingham wanted to visit Colney Heath with his wife. The referral had the blessing of the chairman of the trustees and patron of St Mark's, Canon Arthur Bennett, then rector at Little Munden with Sacombe, near Ware. Acting in the best spirit of the exercise of patronage, he suggested the man deemed to be the best next occupant of the vicarage and one who, distantly, was a relative.

The new vicar was instituted and inducted on 1 December 1980, a few days short of the anniversary of the church's consecration. At 32, he was one of the youngest incumbents to take office at Colney Heath. It was his first living.

Not being 'of marble, brown and veined', the simple wooden pulpit was easy to remove, along with other fitments, ready for re-ordering at St Mark's.

David Veness was born in Tunbridge Wells where he went to school. He was a keen sportsman with a special passion for cricket. If academic work was a struggle sometimes, he nevertheless achieved A-levels, and as a practical person, was attracted to engineering where the emphasis would be on work with hands rather than words. The school leaver went on to secure a place at Brunel University and, in due time, a degree in mechanical engineering. It was while he was an undergraduate that the Christian faith he had embraced in 1964 was put under pressure and later strengthened. His landlord during his college days, the Revd John Pearce, had challenged the aspiring engineer to consider the ordained ministry. The suggestion was taken seriously, but after graduating and, in 1970, marrying, the direction of vocation for David Veness was not at all certain.

Alison Veness was aware of what theological training would demand of her husband. Her late father had been a clergyman and it was after his death that the family moved to Tunbridge Wells. Alison trained to become a state-registered nurse and went on to study midwifery at Hillingdon Hospital, close to Brunel at Uxbridge.

The Venesses then moved to Birmingham. While his wife qualified as a health visitor, David Veness began a two-year period working in industry. In 1972 he was reminded of the call to the ministry, a call first apparent in 1967. The couple moved south and David, who was soon to be ordained, began three years' theological training at St John's College, Nottingham. The principal was Michael Green and David Veness' personal tutor was the Revd Dr George L. Carey, who later became the one hundred and third Archbishop of Canterbury.

The Revd David Veness, deacon, returned to Birmingham to serve at St Stephen's in Selly Oak. A house move and a second curacy ushered in the challenge of converting a church hall into one of three worship centres and seeing the parish double its population to 20,000.

By the time of the move to Colney Heath in December 1980, three young children completed the vicarage family: Jonathan was a very lively four-and-a-half-year-old, Rachel was petite and demure at two and a half, and Andrew was a contented baby of just six months.

Great progress in the church at Colney Heath was seen in the Veness years through to the end of the one hundred and fiftieth anniversary year of the parish. In the vicar's 15 years to the December 1995 celebrations, highlights included the opening of the new Christian Centre – a splendid building that could never have been called a church hall. The church itself underwent complete re-ordering; it became better lit both inside and out and was made more welcoming and a pleasure to enter. The youth work forged ahead spectacularly and Sunday morning services were duplicated to accommodate all those wishing to attend – Horatio Nelson Dudding would surely have rejoiced.

The Revd David Veness remained vicar at Colney Heath for more than two years beyond the one hundred and fiftieth anniversary of the church. He had completed a ministry of 17 years and four months and was 50 years old when he resigned the living in March 1998.

Not before time demolition caught up with the 'temporary' hall.

The new spaciousness of the church's east end.

The accommodation provided for church and village groups to worship and meet in improved environments, has resulted also in a pleasant vista opening up in Church Lane.

Built partly on the site of the old hall, St Mark's Christian Centre has proved to be a greatly appreciated facility for the community.

*A contrast in scenes
between 1901 and 1995.*

Chapter Seven

People & Places

GROUPS & ORGANISATIONS

A list of the secretaries of local organisations is held in the Parish Council Office; the names of some 30 contacts exist and are published occasionally in the *Colney Heath Chronicle*.

Colney Heath Parish Council

Colney Heath Parish Council was established by County Council Order on 15 April 1947 as an independent unit of local government. The interests of Colney Heath and district had, from much earlier times, been in the care of the former St Peter's Rural Parish, which through two electoral wards locally, served both London Colney and Colney Heath.

The name of the Parish Council will remain linked with that of its clerk of 32 years, Mr H. Dudley Wood. His local-government career began in September 1932, when at the age of 17 he started with the former St Albans Rural District Council at their offices in Lattimore Road, St Albans. In 1936 he was appointed part-time clerk to the Parish Council at Sandridge; the same year he qualified as a certified teacher of Pitman's shorthand – a skill to prove its worth at council meetings along with his ability to touch-type the minutes.

Before becoming the clerk at Colney Heath in 1958, Dudley Wood spent the years of the Second World War in the Royal Armoured Corps, seeing

Parish Council clerk, H. Dudley Wood, with Bryan Lilley, the chairman, at the council's first civic service in July 1983.

service in North Africa and Italy and emerging as a company sergeant-major (no wonder he knew how to keep Parish Council meetings on an even keel).

Two significant events happened in 1952: Dudley Wood was appointed deputy clerk to St Albans Rural District Council and, for the princely sum of 10s., the Parish Council purchased from the Earl of Essex a narrow strip of the common fronting the High Street. A similar peppercorn was paid in 1961 to secure the remainder of Colney Heath common in one public ownership, thus making irregular long-staying encampments by travellers easier to deal with under the law.

In 1958, Dudley Wood had decided to relinquish the clerkship at Sandridge after 21 years' service. Then fate took a hand. Colney Heath's parish clerk at that time, Mr A.G. Jenkins, a schoolmaster, died suddenly after an end-of-term cricket match. Dudley Wood was asked to take over temporarily, mainly to get the council's books through the annual audit. It was to be the first audit of many more to come. Finding Colney Heath Parish Council a more harmonious body, the temporary clerk competed for the vacancy and secured the clerkship.

Many firsts for the Parish Council were flagged up in Dudley Wood's tenure of office. In 1959 the Parish Council was instrumental in first signing up the parish for the best kept village competition run by Hertfordshire Society. Over the years many certificates, commendations and awards have been won. Honours have fallen mostly to Tyttenhanger Green in exchange for a lot of hard work by the hamlet community, which represented the parish.

It was in July 1961 that the remaining majority part of the common was vested in the Parish Council thanks to both the Earl of Caledon (Tyttenhanger) and Major General Sir George Burns (North Mymms Park) ceding their ownership. Within a month the Parish Council issued notice that the unofficial encampments which had featured on the common for a long period of years should be removed. A dramatic exodus was made in the glare of national television news and under the persuasion of Barbara Cartland, county councillor and novelist of Essendon. To prevent a return of the travellers, ditches were dug round the common's perimeter.

Very much welcomed was the Commons Registration Act of 1965. The Parish Council immediately registered the ownership and status of the common, together with the village greens at Sleapshyde and Tyttenhanger Green.

May 1972 saw the Parish Council's first woman member to be elected. Councillor Mary Cooper went on to be installed as the council's first female chairman in 1981. In the local government year of 1973/74 Dudley Wood was appointed the last clerk to St Albans Rural District

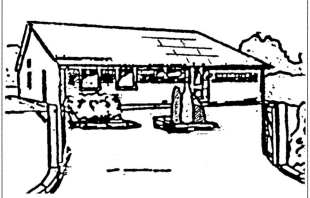

The big event at Tyttenhanger Green in September 1975 was the opening of the Charles Morris Hall. The community building was erected by the Parish Council following years of negotiations to carry out terms of a legacy involving trusteeships and land exchange.

Council, prior to that authority's disappearance under local government re-organisation.

A memorial garden was established in front of the village hall in 1974, marking the death in June of that year of Councillor W.G. 'Bill' Franklin who had served the Council as an elected member since 1949.

There was great rejoicing among the people of Tyttenhanger Green in September 1975 at the official opening of the Charles Morris Hall; it was built by the Parish Council after years of complex paperwork and consultation with local residents. The same month saw publication of the Parish Council's first edition of the *Colney Heath Chronicle*; the magazine was the inspiration of the late councillors Arthur Cutmore and Harry Ward. Dudley Wood became the editor. Other parishes in the district – Harpenden, Redbourn, Sandridge and Wheathampstead – followed with magazines of their own, but Colney Heath's was the first!

Substantial local concern was being mounted early in 1980 for the need or otherwise of the Tollgate Road link from South Hatfield to Bullens Green Lane. The Parish Council called a public meeting and the A1(M) Colney Heath/North Mymms Action Group was formed. Local canvassing unearthed a substantial opposition to the proposed link (except for pedestrians and cyclists) and the scheme was opposed at the March 1981 public inquiry; it was abandoned.

In 1981, the year Mary Cooper became chairman of the Parish Council, came the culmination of the Parish Council's efforts to secure a European twinning partner. An emissary from Boissy-sous-St Yon, a 2800-strong community 20 miles south of Paris, arrived in Colney Heath for discussions and Dudley Wood and his French-speaking daughter made a return trip on behalf of the parish. Later, on 3 December, a presentation

This was the first group photograph taken of the council members and clerk after 35 years of the Parish Council's existence. Pictured, left to right, in the entrance of the old pavilion building on 21 April 1982 are John F. Prodger (then vice chairman), Alan J. Montague, Theo Stuchbery, Ralph W. Page, Mary Cooper, chairman, Bryan K. Lilley, Alex Angelow, and Dudley Wood. Harry J. Ward was absent.

Dudley Wood, the parish council clerk, receives from Bryan Lilley, the chairman, an illuminated address on vellum recording the council's appreciation of Mr Wood's 25 years' service as clerk. On the left is Mrs Margaret Weaver, calligrapher of St Albans who engrossed the special parchment.

A sign at the edge of part of a new community forest, where it is accessible off Whitehorse Lane, proclaims 'The Dudley Wood'. It is a memorial tribute to the former parish council clerk. The special sign was unveiled by Mr Wood's daughter, Jenny.

was made to local organisations and the representatives of village organisations decided to form the Colney Heath/Boissy-sous-St Yon Twinning Association. The first chairman was Dudley Wood.

The year 1982 saw the launch of the Parish Council's best kept front garden competition and also the best kept (parish) community competition. In April of that year there was another first for Colney Heath Parish Council; the members had their first group photograph taken in the council's 35-year history. Standing on the steps of the recreation ground pavilion, those present with the clerk were Councillors John F. Prodger (vice chairman), Alan J. Montague, Theo Stuchbery, Ralph W. Page, Mary Cooper (chairman), Bryan K. Lilley and Alex Angelow. Councillor Harry J. Ward was unavoidably absent. It was thanks to Councillor Stuchbery that members becoming chairman of the Parish Council were able to identify themselves at public events by wearing the council's chairman's badge of office suspended from a double-gilt chain. Councillor Stuchbery made the badge and chain for his colleagues' use following his own period as council chairman.

On 10 July 1983, the incoming chairman, Bryan Lilley, arranged for the council's first parish civic service to take place in St Mark's Church. It was well supported by councillors past and present, district and county councillors, the mayor and mayoress of the City and District of St Albans and by the Member of Parliament, Mr Peter Lilley, and his wife.

December 1983 saw a very special occasion in the Charles Morris Hall; it followed the two hundred and seventy fifth meeting of the Parish Council with Dudley Wood as its clerk. In other words it marked his twenty-fifth anniversary in office as the council's chief executive officer. There had never before been such a packed hall for a council meeting. Parish councillors past and present paid tribute to their clerk's sterling service. On behalf of the council, the chairman, Councillor Bryan Lilley, presented Dudley Wood with an illuminated address on vellum that recorded a resolution of the Parish Council in appreciation of his dedication and commitment to the service of Colney Heath Parish.

In presenting the vellum (the work of calligrapher Mrs Margaret Weaver of St Albans) the chairman told Dudley Wood:

The Parish Council thanks you for not only the public work you do so efficiently but also for the vast amount of unseen work that you undertake and have done so willingly for these past 25 years, branching out into the life of Colney Heath Parish. We are very fortunate.

During his remaining years in post, Dudley Wood completed a lot more work; he served a total of 32 years as clerk. The council and community were stunned in 1991 to learn of his disappearance without trace while on holiday with his family in the Azores. In 1992 a former playing field on the parish border in Whitehorse Lane was planted by the County Council with native trees, such as cherry, hornbeam and oak. This one hectare of woodland – to be part of the Watling Chase Community Forest – has been dedicated to the memory of Colney Heath's much missed energetic parish clerk.

There was a happy occasion in November 1997 when the woodland's sign, The Dudley Wood, was unveiled by the former clerk's daughter, Jenny. The honouring of Dudley was most appropriate, and possessed of his great sense of humour, he would surely have appreciated the play on words.

Mrs Caroline Pluck succeeded Dudley Wood as parish clerk and the clerk at the time of writing is Debra Mayhew, assisted by Loraine Wenham. They operate from the parish office attached to the modern extension to the village hall.

The Methodist Chapel, Sleapshyde

The Methodists were well established in the district before the parish church was built. The Wesleyan community initially gathered together in a house that was gradually enlarged, and ultimately took the form of the present chapel. It was natural that the growing, active and nonconformist congregation chose to locate their place of worship at Sleapshyde, a hamlet first mentioned in a thirteenth-century manuscript. Here the tight-knit community was thriving and the area had a far greater number of cottage homes than those spread along the High Street at Colney Heath.

The Wesleyan Methodists were meeting in private homes in Sleapshyde by 1835 – ten years before the parish church opened. Six years on, the pioneer chapel was built 'in lieu of a cottage'. The first minister was the Revd M. Britton and the new building was to accommodate over 100 worshippers. Outside 'tethering for horses' was provided.

Methodist chapels at this time, like parish churches, came to the attention of William Upton's famous religious survey of 1847–51. The comments arose from his 'observed behaviour' in most of the Methodist places of worship in Hertfordshire. At their most pointed, both churches and chapels came in for colourful comments such as: 'all depraved people', 'people dull and ignorant', 'vicar immoral', 'preacher illiterate' and 'congregation larger when preacher away'.

The chapel's holy table was given in memory of Mr Arthur Smith who served the fellowship for many years as children's superintendent. He was a natural leader and friend who also served as a JP on the St Albans magistrates bench. The cross on the table is in memory of Mr Swain, of Wilkins Green Farm; the flower stand in memory of Mr and Mrs Herbert Dickinson; and the lectern was given in memory of Mr Malcolm Tomkins, writer and local historian.

Goodbye and thank you! Chapel members gathered to say farewell to their minister, the Revd David Glover and his wife Dorothy (left) when they exchanged the local circuit for duties with churches in Chesham. Among those present: Mrs Gwen Dickinson, Mrs Joy Tomkins, Mrs Maureen Cox, Mrs Margaret Silsby, Mrs Freda Moore and Keiran Green.

Left: *The chapel's simple entrance porch welcomes those calling in during a local mission.*

Below: *A rarity at Sleapshyde Methodist Chapel – and that's not just the Victorian post box set in the wall outside! The wedding of local bridegroom, Martin Silsby, and Stella from Sri Lanka in June 2000 was only the third marriage ceremony to be conducted in the chapel since 1841. The first ceremony was for John and Margaret (née Lane) Silsby while the second was that of Sharon Marlborough and Roger Barton, whose home is in the High Street, Colney Heath.*

The much-loved little chapel at Sleapshyde is more than a place for worship; as well as ministering to the needs of the soul it offers the community a great deal through a wide range of services and activities. There are flower shows, 'tea and bun' open days, pastoral care, services for the bereaved, baptisms, days for quiet reflection, guest speakers and much more besides.

Of all that Sleapshyde Methodist Chapel stands for, its ministry is particularly valued for the unpretentious acts that take place in the chapel building. It is a place worked generously by the dedicated few, who provide willingly for the needs of the many.

The Revd Laurence Bomford (vicar of Colney Heath 1898–1918) paid generous tribute to the Methodist fellowship when he resigned the living. In a letter to the *Herts Advertiser* he wrote:

No doubt Colney Heath was much neglected by the Church of England in 1842 and the adjoining times; so were many other outlying villages. I am not a Wesleyan, but, for that very reason, it seems to me very unwise that the efforts of the Wesleyans should be entirely ignored... I always found that the best and most religious of the families in Colney Heath parish owed their hopeful condition directly or indirectly to those Wesleyan efforts.

It has often been said that the chapel's heart is larger than its body. That was true when the worship and mission began at that very first meeting of Methodists in Sleapshyde, and it is still true 165 years on – one year short of the 2003 tercentenary of the birth in the Rectory at Epworth, Lincolnshire of John Wesley, whose vision and faith began a great work.

Colney Heath Football Club

Founded in 1907, the 'Magpies' have earned themselves a creditable record over the years. Although achievement on the pitch may not always have been outstanding, the club has strengthened as an organisation, contributing significantly to providing a focal point in Colney Heath for motivated sportsmen to follow in the best traditions of the amateur game. The club is an old-established, but far from old-fashioned, institution. As a sports organisation, it comes second in foundation terms, however, to the cricket club started soon after the arrival in 1898 of a keen all-round player, Laurence George Bomford, who was Colney Heath's seventh vicar.

Colney Heath Football Club is a survivor organisation. It has had its peaks and troughs; stalwarts have remained loyal and the playing and clubhouse facilities have improved dramatically in recent years. It is all a far cry from the spartan days of matches on the Fuzzen (furze) field and the football of the Hatfield and District League where the third and fourth teams still play.

There were honours in the foundation year, as the club competed for the North Mymms Charity Cup. However, it was some time before the team achieved much further success, this time in the Mid Herts League in the 1935–36 season. Soon the disruption years of the war arrived. Potential players were among the 22 young men of Colney Heath who did not return from the hostilities of the Second World War.

Every club has its day. The golden era of football for the 'Magpies' was from 1946 through to 1960. In this period the club won the Mid Herts Benevolent Shield twice, plus the Bingham Cox Cup and the Division One and Premier Division titles. In 1952 the club was relocated to the High Street Recreation Ground. Facilities then were somewhat limited, and although the old pavilion represented an improvement of sorts, the interior was less than inviting. Despite this, the club got on with the job in hand and successes followed one after the other; it won two Playing Fields cups, as well as the Aubrey Cup twice, plus Division Two, Division One and Premiership titles. The culmination in 1960 was the Herts Intermediate Cup and Aubrey Cup double. The Reserve side also completed a double in 1958, winning both Cup and League titles. Less exciting trophies were picked up between the 1960s and the 1980s but, on the whole, these were pretty fallow years on the field.

In the mid 1980s the club achieved giant strides of improvements both on and off the field. These were driven largely by the need to meet new standards required by the Herts County League; achievement of the standards in every respect will pave the way for club entry to the national FA Vase via South Midlands football. Reaching the last 128 so far illustrates the reality of the task.

Delicate negotiations opened during this time between club officials and Colney Heath Parish Council over improvements at the High Street ground. Bizarrely, somebody suggested that the old air-raid shelter, converted to garages and a store, which stood in the car park, might make a clubhouse! Much lateral thinking took place and it was ultimately the Parish Council that decided to free up greater access to the pavilion by leasing it to the football club. It was the right decision. Almost immediately the club had the kitchen modernised, the place re-decorated and some of the pavilion carpeted. Things were set to improve further but major interior alterations and a planned external facelift had to take a different course following 15 August 1988, when the clubhouse burnt down.

The rebuilding was tackled with a renewed sense of purpose and the club's 200-strong membership soon rose to 300. The new building gives a fleeting reminder of the old, with its wooden cladding, but inside there is no comparison with what stood before. The club is now equipped to a higher standard than ever; it is able to entertain visiting players and officials in comfortable surroundings and the social club members enjoy greater comfort. Colney Heath has gained a first-class facility. The financial security that the social club provides has enabled the parent football club to maintain the pitch to the standards the game requires.

Despite the trauma of the fire and consequently being without a clubhouse, the real business of playing football continued. Using a portakabin as their temporary base, the 'Magpies' gained entry to the Premier Division. The new clubhouse was completed in 1989 and by 1993 an extension was added along with post and rails. The floodlights were erected in February 2000.

109

Colney Heath Football Club champs of Coronation Year 1952–53.

Back row left to right: *Ernie Perry, Bill Rhodes, Tony Wilson, Brian Stoker,*
Monty Tomlinson, Reg Simpkins, John Wilmott, Roy Turner, Jack Matthews, John Marsling,
Derek Seabrook, Vic Hodgkins;
middle row: *Jesse Saywell, Angus Davies, Basil Stoker, Ron Littlechild, Jimmy Dawes,*
Doofy Clayton, Johnny Walker;
front row: *Ted Wilson, Ernie Ralph, Charlie Hill, Ronnie Eacott.*

Winners: First division Mid-Herts Intermediate League;
Division 1 Mid-Herts League; St Albans Playing Fields Cup.

Entry to South Midlands football eluded the club between 1994–98 with third- and fourth-place finishes when second place would have been enough. Centenary trophies back to back and another Aubrey Cup were won, finally heralding the coveted Championship in 2000. The club came from 15 points behind in January to beat rivals, Wormley, by ten points.

Looking back, the club records show that competitions won by the First XI in the years around the wars are more recently often won by the Third XI – a debating point at the bar if ever there was one.

Ladies football started at Colney Heath in 1993. The two teams play in the Greater London Premier Division against the likes of Chelsea, Spurs and West Ham, and they are among the top 80 teams in the country. Additionally, the youth team development programme started in 1994 and provides football and enjoyment for over 60 boys who regularly use the club's facilities.

Colney Heath Football Club has developed and strengthened over the years. Its success is the story of partnership and interdependence. The officials, players, sponsors, supporters and social club members have all done much, collectively and individually, to make Colney Heath FC a name both known and respected in Hertfordshire football. Long may it continue.

The Women's Institute

Colney Heath Women's Institute was formed in Coronation Year 1953 under the presidency of Mrs Madge Behling. Two remarkable founder members – Mrs Kath Marlborough and Mrs Kate Butcher – still find time to attend every monthly meeting. In July 2001 Mrs Butcher's ninetieth birthday was celebrated in great style and she was honoured with flowers presented on behalf of the 34 members at the time. The institute's membership record stood at more than 80.

The WI has long been pro-active in village events of all kinds. For several years members organised the popular produce show, and with the enthusiasm of the members, in conjunction with the Village Hall Council, it also arranged the senior citizens' party each February. This great army of 'doers' at the heart of social life in Colney Heath put on shows to raise money for new curtain material for the village hall and, as if that was not enough, then made all the curtains for the stage, windows and doors. Carol singing round the houses in aid of various good causes has been another annual activity, and a free alfresco party to celebrate the fiftieth anniversary of VE Day was a worthy one-off.

The WI has always been ready to lend total support for events arranged by other village organisations. The record is a fine one; members regularly helped at the baby clinic in the old recreation ground pavilion and they delivered the Parish Council Christmas parcels. They are still professionals when it comes to providing refreshments on special occasions, such as the opening of the village hall extension and the official declaration of the common as a site of special scientific interest.

Village Day owes much of its success to the part played by the WI. In the early years the task was providing teas for adults and free sticky buns for the children, as well as 2s.6d. (the equivalent of 12½ pence in modern money) in national savings stamp prizes for the race winners. More recently the favourite money-spinner has been the popular bottle tombola.

In a memorable visual history of the parish that was performed by the WI, a narrator led the audience around a series of animated tableaux, each of which depicted an aspect in the development of Colney Heath. Two WI members were dressed as chickens – a fact that nobody has dared even to ask about since!

The organisation has also been involved in activities outside the parish: the WI Choir has featured on television and a crack quiz team reached the final in a knockout competition that was broadcast on the radio. All sorts of skills have blossomed including creating the most spectacular prize-winning floats in St Albans Carnival. On top of all this, the members have also demonstrated their abilities at punting, gliding and even clay-pigeon shooting.

All in all, the village would certainly be the poorer without the ladies of the WI. A toast to them all – and not a word about jam nor, for that matter, Jerusalem!

Happy, smiling faces of WI members at Colney Heath. This busy team prepared refreshments at the official opening on 13 May 2000 of the extension to the village hall. Left to right: Mrs Sylvia Kendleton, Gerry Savage, Mrs Joan Ison, Mrs Mary Collins, Mrs June Cain, Mrs Marion Thompson, Mrs Nancy Taffs and Mrs Doreen Sellar.

Salute to six of the 1953 founder WI members at this reunion gathering in 1982.
Left to right: Mrs Kath Marlborough, Mrs Dorothy Sainty, Mrs Kate Butcher,
Mrs Emily Smith, Mrs Amy Richardson and Mrs Sybil Pickett

Watch out – the girls from St Trinians are about!
Mo Butler and Maggie Wilson, two stalwart and
good-hearted Colney Heath members helped win
prizes for the WI float at St Albans carnival.
The 'jolly hockey sticks' Maggie hid her WI
Madam President identity behind the dark glasses!

The Twinning Association

After the end of the Second World War, town twinning associations were rapidly established across Europe as a means of re-establishing and improving links between countries. Dudley Wood, the post-war clerk of the newly independent Colney Heath Parish Council, was keen to get involved. He was instrumental in seeking out a suitable continental community similar in size and profile to that of Colney Heath and Smallford.

It was not until 1981, however, that Colney Heath was twinned with Boissy-sous-St Yon, south of Paris. Dudley Wood became the first chairman of the twinning association established between the two communities. He very quickly used his contacts – and not a little charm – to establish a lively organisation that consisted of a membership of all ages, to further the cause of the twinning vision. There could not have been a better founding chairman.

Strong and lasting friendships quickly grew between families in Colney Heath and Boissy. Some interesting French personalities were introduced to their UK counterparts. Local families and individuals are often invited to Boissy for holidays and family events such as weddings. They are also invited to take part in a variety of community-based festivals and celebrations.

When Dudley Wood resigned as chairman his place was taken by Alan King, who continued in office until early 2001. Over the years, the annual reunions held alternately in Colney Heath and Boissy have always been well supported. Activities like barbecues, dinner-dances, quiz nights and boules competitions take place in Colney Heath in order to promote the Twinning Association and to raise funds. Membership in both Boissy and Colney Heath continues to flourish and grow – towards a united Europe!

Above left: *Dudley Wood, founder chairman of the Twinning Association, entered into the spirit of things on the association's float in Colney Heath village day carnival procession.* Above middle: *In the May 1999 well-ordered exchange across the English Channel, the mayor of Boissy, M. Meysonnier (right with cycle) pedalled the 600km to Colney Heath with Boissy twinning member, M. Mazouin. They and their wives are greeted by the out-going chairman and the 2002 president of Colney Heath Twinning Association.* Above right: *One of the younger members of the visiting Colney Heath 'twinners' delights in reaching Boissy.*

When Colney Heath hosted the Boissy twinning visitors in 2001 everyone enjoyed a sight-seeing trip to London.

Colney Heath's Senior Citizens

Colney Heath does not naturally admit to having old folk. Rather, it has the more user friendly and inclusive 'older people' and they are the life and soul of the place! Most find great pleasure in being associated with two amazing local organisations – Colney Heath Day Care Centre, now 16 years old; and the happy forum established over 50 years ago, the Old Friends' Club. The two organisations have served the village's senior community with dedication over the years, and while their programmes and aims are distinctive, they have often shared the same membership.

For the last ten years or so, the Old Friends have had as their organising secretary Mr I.L. Walker. Members continue to meet regularly on the first and third Mondays of the month to enjoy a varied programme of activities, outings and lunches. The membership of the club in 2002 is around 50.

There has always been a very good relationship between Old Friends' Club members and the children of the primary school; very often club members have been the delighted recipients of gifts of fruit and vegetables donated by the youngsters as part of the school's harvest festival celebrations.

The Day Care Centre's energetic co-ordinator for the last ten years or so has been Mr Fred Olver, who took over from Mrs Jean Hacker. However, at the time of writing Mr Olver had recently decided that although he will continue to give his support to the worthy venture, he feels a younger person should be at the helm, in order to revitalise the complex inter-dependent administration of the centre, which is capable of offering great support to a largely elderly clientele.

The Day Care Centre in Colney Heath opened in October 1986 as one of a number established by county Social Services in the St Albans area under the inspired direction of Mrs June Pettifer. The Christian centre at St Mark's Church has offered the clients and teams of voluntary helpers ideal facilities. At the time of the foundation of the centre, Mr Olver assisted as treasurer, while Ann Bates was secretary. The role from the beginning was to provide care and companionship as well as meals for elderly residents of Colney Heath, Sleapshyde, Smallford and Oaklands.

A door-to-door pick-up service was established to provide access for all to the centre's regular Thursday meetings; many members appreciated the ambulance transport, fitted with a tail-lift to accommodate wheelchairs. Many local organisations contributed generously to help equip the centre.

A typical day at the centre starts with a welcome cup of tea or coffee. A break in activities in the middle of the day heralds a delicious lunch, cooked in the school kitchen. The day's programme invariably ends with tea and home-made cake provided by one of the helpers. Craft group activities, started by Mr Frank Morris, prove very popular, and members enjoy making a wide variety of items for sale to family and friends. Day Centre members from London Colney often join in the afternoon activities when entertainers visit Colney Heath.

The key to success for the Day Care Centre is being able to rely on a willing band of volunteers. A new drive for renewed help was underway at the time of writing, which with the encouragement and support of key local organisations, should result in the continuation of the much-needed service that benefits the elderly house-bound of Colney Heath and district.

Members of Colney Heath Old Friends' Club enjoyed the celebrations in the village hall marking the 50th anniversary of VE-Day.

Above: *Members and helpers of the Day Care Centre at their Christmas party in St Mark's Christian Centre.*

Right: *It was Easter bonnet making day for the ladies at this springtime meeting of Day Care Centre members.*

A perfect summer outing – Day Care Centre members and friends enjoy a tour of the National Rose Society grounds at Chiswell Green.

Colney Heath Village Hall

It all started on 23 September 1936 when the Declaration of Trust for the Village Hall was made by the Council of the parish of St Peter Rural (now Colney Heath Parish Council). Mr Roland Richardson, headmaster at the school and a prime mover in much of Colney Heath's community life, applied on behalf of the council, to the Ministry of Agriculture and Fisheries to construct the hall on the piece of common land on which it now stands. The building was erected by local voluntary labour and was opened to the public for the first time in December 1938. It was a triumph of local endeavour.

Although the Trustees were the Council of the parish, the Trust declaration decreed that the hall should be managed and controlled by a Council of Management formed from organisations in the village and by users of the hall. This policy continues to apply. Originally, it was intended that there should be representatives from no more than 12 organisations but the Council of Management had powers of co-option. Some of the original organisations no longer exist in the village but others have taken their place.

Small but significant improvements to the building have been made over the years. In 1977 toilet facilities that met the necessary standards for use by disabled people were installed just inside the main entrance. The most significant and welcome structural change was the completion of the millennium extension. This was officially opened on 13 May 2000 by Councillor Mike Morrell, Mayor of the City and District of St Albans. The extension comprises a new kitchen, added to the eastern side of the hall, behind which is the Parish Council office and a new community room. A second WC built to disabled use standards has been added in this area, and the rear of the hall has been extended to provide more storage space behind the stage.

On its foundation, the purpose of the hall was that it should be used for education, relaxation, sport, leisure and social events for the benefit of the village community. The original village organisations represented on the Council of Management in 1936 were: Colney Heath British Legion branch and the Women's Section, Loyal Hope Lodge, Colney Heath Football Club, St Mark's PCC, Colney Heath Nursing Association, St Peter's Parish Council (Colney Heath Ward), the Trustees of Sleapshyde Methodist Chapel, the Men's Committee, the school managers and the Mothers' Union.

The policy of inclusion has continued to dominate the hall's activities. Indeed, few local people miss the highlight event: the New Year party hosted by the Village Hall Committee. The WI also help to organise this event and provide the entertainment, aided by schoolteacher, Mr Peter Jessop, at the piano.

A short walk from the village hall brings interest in the shape of these London coal duty boundary markers. Introduced in 1851, some 45 were set up around South Hertfordshire after 1861. They mark the outer limits of the metropolitan area, showing that when consignments of coal destined for London passed the boundary a duty tax was payable.

Colney Heath has four of the markers. Located on or close to the common, the white-painted, square, cast-iron squat columns carry the arms of the City of London – the red St George's cross quartered with the sword of St Paul. Some of the markers carry a plate screwed on to the shaft referring to the Act of Parliament authorising the setting up of the boundary post. Using regnal years identity, the plate reads: 24 & 25 VICT. CAP 42 signifying the 24th and 25th year of the reign of Queen Victoria and the 42nd chapter of the Act.

The tax earned by the duty payable by hauliers of coal helped fund a wide range of services from the government and national provisions to subsidising the redecoration costs of St Paul's Cathedral.

Colney Heath's four coal duty posts, numbered left, together with the OS grid references are (1) TL 199 059 North of the river, close to the Church Lane bridge; (2) TL205 058 best preserved post north of Coursers Road near the Queen's Head; (3) TL 205 050 north of the farm, at the bend, south side of Coursers Road; (4) TL 205 059 on the common opposite the Cock public house.

Scouts and Guides

The uniformed organisations continue to flourish in Colney Heath and meet regularly in their own headquarters building set in Roestock playing fields.

It was soon after the arrival in Colney Heath of the twelfth vicar – the Revd W.E. Butland – that the Scout and Guide movements were re-kindled following a time of decline. The intention had been that the uniformed groups, like the flourishing Church Lads' Brigade and Church Girls' Brigade before them, might also become church affiliated. Mrs Butland started a new Guide company in 1959, with Miss Joan Montague in charge of the Brownies. Scouts followed with Mr Douglas Beard as Scoutmaster and Mrs Elaine Beard as the Cubs' Akela.

All these constituent groups (including the Cub Scouts and the Beavers) were given a good start in the inadequate church hall, with its limited storage space. Eventually, the group as a whole elected to become entirely secular and transferred to their own more comfortable, purpose-built headquarters at Roestock.

Above left: *A parade day for Colney Heath's Guides and Brownies; the company and pack were given a new start in 1959 when they met in the old church hall.*

Above right: *Three new Guides at their enrolment ceremony.*

Left: *A young Brownie chosen to carry the pack flag on church parade day.*

Left: *In for a soaking during the crowd-pulling bed race on Village Day.*

Below: *An apprehensive start for the youngest competitors on sports day in 1974.*

Bottom: *The 1977 Queen's Silver Jubilee celebrated at the old pavilion on the recreation ground.*

Postscript

Invariably it is a mistake to analyse too soon what counts for progress in any situation, let alone in a story spanning 150 years. Attempting to measure a community's progress is as difficult a task, say, as trying to dissect the countless sermons preached in church and chapel at Colney Heath. Like Sunday lunches, sermons, while they are appreciated, may not always be remembered for very long after the event. The recall of any one may become decidedly hazy, yet sermons and good Sunday lunches have something in common: they share the highly desirable effect, over time, of building both body and soul, however remiss the recipient may be about acknowledging the benefits.

Clearly, not everything in the parish of Colney Heath has been plain sailing through these 150 momentous years. There have been some upsets and storms as well as the 'calm sea and prosperous voyage'. The last 40 years, particularly, have seen the community coping with enormous pressures. These have consumed the nation state and borne down upon families and individuals alike.

Past is indeed prologue. However, it must often be conceded that the past is a good servant but a poor master. There are valuable lessons to be learned from the past about the life and times of the people of Colney Heath Parish.

From the Second World War to the end of the twentieth century, many of those passing through the village – or remaining there – have at some point or another found time in their lives for their church or chapel. This account of the Colney Heath story was inspired by the events leading to and following the laying of the foundation stone of the parish church in the spring of 1845. Since that time the people have been renewed by the continuing and inextinguishable hope of the Easter message. There has been good cause, too, to be mindful of the service of the clergy over the years in which this history has been annotated. Particularly, great sacrifice was demonstrated by the *triumvirate* of incumbents who served at the end of the sesquicentenary of Colney Heath. It remains a vibrant ecclesiastical parish.

Laus Deo.

Appendices

BISHOPS WITH OVERSIGHT OF COLNEY HEATH 1845–1995

Bishop of London
1845   Charles James Blomfield

Bishops of Rochester
1846   George Murray
1860   Joseph Cotton Wigram
1867   Thomas Legh Claughton

Bishops of St Albans
1877   Thomas Legh Claughton
1890   John Festing
1903   Edgar Jacob
1920   Michael Furse
1945   Philip Loyd
1950   Edward Michael Gresford-Jones
1970   Robert Alexander Kennedy Runcie
1980   John Bernard Taylor
1995   Christopher Herbert (enthroned 20 January 1996)

CHURCHWARDENS

In the following list, the dates given are the first of unbroken consecutive years' service:

        Mark Tarry
        John Thomas Patience (14 years in office)
        Charles Morris
        Charles Jolly
1902   James C. Simmons
1919   Reginald C. Hart-Dyke
1919   Harry John Selborne Boome (14 years)
1926   Thomas Halliwell
        Walter H. Sherriff
1928   William Gordon Muir
1930   Richard S. Robertson
1933   Alfred M. Dickinson
1934   Howard F. Taylor
1937   Christopher E. Tarry
1941   H.J. Selborne Boome
        Miss Louisa S. Edwards
1947   T. Halliwell (42 years)
1953   J.E. Parnell
1960   Bryan Harrison
        A. Briggs
1961   H.W. Jelley
1964   Richard I. Ostler

1969   Bernard Bruton
1981   David Dimmick
1974   David Vesey
1975   Clifford Harvey
1979   Bryan Kenneth Lilley
1980   Stephen Shaw
1982   Norah Marshall
1985   John Stansfeld
1987   Paul Mason
1988   Peter Halden
1992   Stephen Charlwood
1995   Ian Downs

VERGERS

Thomas Halliwell (for 42 years)
Violet Lily Halliwell, née Wilson (for 38 years)

READERS

Anthony David Trevor Gorton
Mrs E.A. (Jenny) James

ASSISTANT CLERGY

1871   Revd Edward M. Farley
1972   Revd John Melville Scutt
1981   Revd Anthony D. T. Gorton
1987   Revd Brian Richard McMahon

PAROCHIAL CHURCH COUNCIL/CHURCH SECRETARIES

1932   G. Gordon Cooper
              Miss Louisa S. Edwards
1970   Mrs Mary Collins
1971–74   Mrs Mavis Maslin
1975   Mrs Sue Vesey
1976–78   Mrs Sheila Dimmick
1979   Leonard Marshall
1980   Sam McAnlis
              Leonard Thresher
1980–86   Mrs Norah Marshall
1987   Mrs Judy Smith

ELECTORAL ROLL KEEPER

1971–2002   Mrs Mary Collins

VICAR'S SECRETARY

1983–   Mrs Judy Smith

CHURCH REGISTERS

Registers of Baptisms
*Volume I	800 entries:	31 January 1847 – 26 January 1879
*Volume II	800 entries:	26 January 1879 – 27 September 1908
*Volume III	800 entries:	27 September 1908 – 23 May 1943
Volume IV	800 entries:	11 July 1943 – 8 January 1978
Volume V	800 entries:	7 May 1978 – (current at 31 December 1995)

Registers of Marriage
*Volume I	500 entries:	29 November 1847 – 12 March 1938
*Volume II	100 entries:	18 April 1938 – 16 April 1949

*Volume III	100 entries:	17 April 1949 – 20 June 1959
*Volume IV	100 entries:	27 June 1959 – 30 March 1968
*Volume V	50 entries:	29 June 1968 – 11 November 1972
*Volume VI	50 entries:	9 December 1972 – 20 September 1980
*Volume VII	50 entries:	25 October 1980 – 14 June 1986
*Volume VIII	50 entries:	12 July 1986 – 23 November 1991
Volume IX	50 entries:	4 April 1992 – 2 September 2000

Registers of Burials

*Volume I	800 entries:	26 December 1846 – 28 February 1911
Volume II	800 entries:	11 April 1911 – 27 June 1958
Volume III	800 entries:	30 June 1958 – (current at 31 December 1995)

Registers of Services

*Four volumes:	1891 – 1914
	1914 – 1929
	1930 – 1946
	1969 – 1979

Miscellaneous

*PCC Minutes	1937 – 1960
	1961 – 1970
*Accounts	1918 – 1926
	1926 – 1933
	1941 – 1953
	1954 – 1967
*Cash Book	1936 – 1961

Volumes marked * are lodged with the St Albans Diocesan Archives held at the County Record Office, County Hall, Hertford SG13 8DE.

MONUMENTS AND MEMORIALS WITHIN THE CHURCH

North Wall

1. Marble plaque: *In loving memory of John Thomas Patience of Popefield, St Albans. Died 12 May 1903, aged 64. 40 years regular attendant and 14 years churchwarden of this church. This tablet is placed here by his widow. Also in remembrance of Eliza Ann, widow of the above, who died 27 June 1923, aged 86 years.*

2. Brass plaque: *In loving memory of Eliza Margretta Harrison, 16 March 1932. Erected by her husband, sons and daughter.*

East wall

3. Alabaster plaque: The First World War, 1914–18. See Chapter 5 for names and details.

4. Alabaster plaque: Second World War memorial. See Chapter 5 for names and details.

5. Brass plaque: The post-1945 memorial to the fallen. See Chapter 5 for more details.

The Sanctuary

6. Central lancet of the east window: The Ascension. *To the Glory of God and in loving memory of the Revd William Bailey and Mary Martin Bailey. Erected by their eldest son in 1925.*

South Wall

7.   Above the vestry entrance: the St Michael window. *To the Glory of God and in loving memory of Joshua Harmon East, died 10 April 1882 and of his son, Edmund James, died 20 September 1929. Donated by the wife and mother.*

8.   Wooden plaque. *To the Glory of God and in remembrance of 14 years' faithful service as churchwarden by Harry John Selborne Boome. The church was electrically lighted by members of the church and friends in March 1934.*

9.   Brass plate. *The fund for the erection of a clock in the tower of the church was initiated by the late Nathaniel Everett Green, artist and astronomer. A humble follower of our Lord and Master and grateful student of His works. As a memorial to him the fund was completed and the clock erected by his relatives, friends, pupils and Sunday scholars, 1901.*

10.   The Good Shepherd window. *To the Glory of God and in memory of Kate Mary, the beloved wife of William Henry Bailey. Erected 1925.*

11.   Alabaster plaque. *In lasting memory of Lawrence George Bomford MA, Vicar of Colney Heath 1898–1918 (born 6 August 1847, died 2 July 1926) and of Anne Goold, his wife and fellow worker (the daughter of N.E. Green) died 6 March 1908, aged 60.*

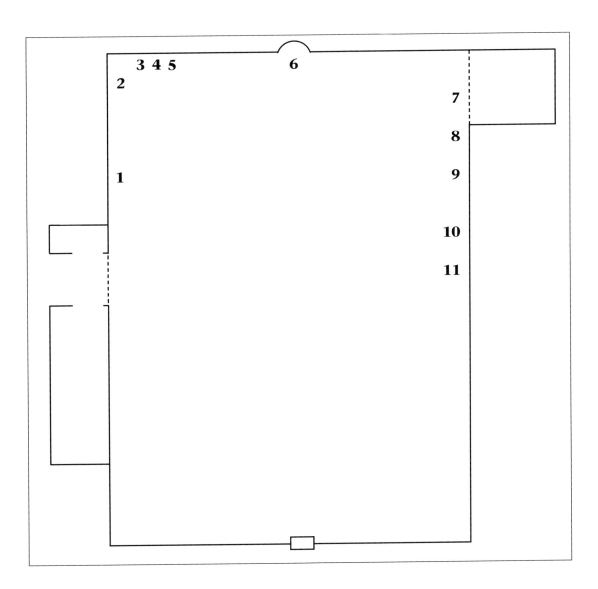

Bibliography

Unpublished sources

Papers from St Mark, Colney Heath Parish Chest 1842–1995 (Diocesan Archives)
The Bishop of London's Records 1845 (The Guildhall Library, City of London)
The Caledon Papers (Herts County Record Office)
Colney Heath Parish Council records
Log books and other records about Colney Heath School

Official Histories

The Life of Field Marshal Earl Alexander of Tunis – Nigel Nicholson
British Security Service Operations 1909–1945 – Nigel West
The Story of Salisbury Hall – Sir George Bellew, Garter King of Arms (1960)
The Cecils of Hatfield House – David Cecil

Published books

Great Nast Hyde – British Aerospace Corporation
The Upper Colne and Colney Heath Common – Colney Heath and District Local History Society
Colney Heath Chronicle – Colney Heath Parish Council
History of Hertfordshire – Cussans
The 100th year of the Cathedral City and Diocese of St Albans – Festalban 77
No voice from the Hall – John Harris
Vol. 25 Nos 138, 139 and 140 – Hertfordshire Countryside
Colney Heath – Hertfordshire Monumental Inscriptions – Herts Family & Population History Society
London Colney Parish Council – London Colney News
The Buildings of England – Hertfordshire – Nikolaus Pevsner
The Buildings of England – Middlesex – Nikolaus Pevsner
Heritage of Britain – A.L. Rowse
Cathedral & City (St Albans) – Robert Runcie (ed.)
The Victorian Diocese – Owen Chadwick
The Victorian City – Asa Briggs
The Future of the Diocese – Robert Runcie
The Hatfield and St Albans Branch of the Great Northern Railway – Roger D. Taylor/Brian Anderson
Hertfordshire – St Peter's – Victoria County History

Subscribers

Sue and Ian Ackroyd, St Albans, Hertfordshire

Brenda and Peter Ackroyd, Oaklands,
Colney Heath

Jenny Allaway, Minehead, Somerset

Delma L. Allen, Smallford, Hertfordshire

Norman Allen, Smallford, Hertfordshire

Malcolm and Lynda Archer, Colney Heath,
Hertfordshire

Mrs Jean Arnold, Colney Heath, Hertfordshire

Edward K. Arnold, London Colney, Hertfordshire

Michael and Marguerite Asker, Caunton, Newark,
Nottinghamshire

Ken Bacon, Colney Heath, Hertfordshire

Julia Bashford, Boissy Close, Hertfordshire

George M. Beach, Sleapshyde, Hertfordshire

Mary F. Beach, Sleapshyde, Hertforshire

William R. Beach, Sleapshyde, Hertfordshire

Irene Beach, Colney Heath, Hertfordshire

Leonard E.J. Bean, Colney Heath, Hertfordshire

Jean and Denis Becker, High Street,
Colney Heath, Hertfordshire

John W. Bell, London Colney, Hertfordshire

Sylvia Blundell (née Armstrong), Colney Heath,
Hertfordshire

Andrew and Rachel Blythe, Colney Heath,
Hertfordshire

John L. Boote, Colney Heath, Hertfordshire

David W. Boote, Colney Heath, Hertfordshire

John Bowles, Blackheath, London

Lauren Bracey, Colney Heath, Hertfordshire

Ken Bracey

Mr Derrick Bridges, Barnet

Jon Brindle, Hatfield, Hertfordshire

Marie E. Brown, Smallford, Hertfordshire

Peter Brown, Colney Heath, Hertfordshire

Neil Brunning, Gainsborough, Lincs.

Colin Brutey, North Mymms, Hertfordshire

John and Linda Burton, Colney Heath,
Hertfordshire

Mr Gary M. Bush, Colney Heath, Hertfordshire

Mr John W.J. Bush, Colney Heath, Hertfordshire

Miss Sheryl M. Bush

Sheila Bush, Sleapshyde Lane

Godfrey Butland, Liverpool

Peter and June Cain, Colney Heath, Hertfordshire

Keith E.J. Canfield, Smallford, Hertfordshire

Beryl and Bernard Carpenter, Sleaps Hyde,
Hertfordshire

David and Gaynor Carroll, St Albans,
Hertfordshire

Maureen Carroll, Colney Heath, Hertfordshire

Ann E. Christie, Colney Heath, Hertfordshire

Bernice Chuck, Hatfield, Hertfordshire

The Clark Family, Colney Heath, Hertfordshire

Gerry Cloke, Colney Heath, Hertfordshire

Colney Heath School and Nursery

Mr and Mrs A. Costa-McFadden

Graham Cutmore, Colney Heath, Hertfordshire

Mr Peter Day

Jonathan Day, Colney Heath, Hertfordshire

Lorely and John Day, Colney Heath,
Hertfordshire

Diana Devereux, St Albans, Hertfordshire

Mrs Duncan, Colney Heath, Hertfordshire

Ken and Sheila Ebsworth, Colney Heath,
Hertfordshire

Sue, Allan, Charlie and Tom Edwards,
Colney Heath, Hertfordshire

Emerson/de Vos, Hill End, Hertfordshire

Ruth Farmer, St Albans, Hertfordshire

Mrs A. Fowler

Ruth Fox (née Lilley), Sleaford, Lincolnshire

W. Roy Franklin, Tollgate, Colney Heath,
Hertfordshire

Mr and Mrs D.L. Franklin, Colney Heath,
Hertfordshire

Ryan and Leanne Franklin-Smith,
Roundhouse Farm

SUBSCRIBERS

Terry and Maureen Franklin-Smith,
  Roundhouse Farm
Carolyn Frost, Colney Heath School
Mark T. Gandolfi, Colney Heath, Hertfordshire
Nigel Gibbins, Colney Heath, Hertfordshire
S.E. Gilbert, Colney Heath, Hertfordshire
Gilson/Brownin, Colney Heath, Hertfordshire
Stephen J. Gore, Tyttenhanger, Hertfordshire
Christine Gowens, Hill End, St Albans,
  Hertfordshire
Peter Gower, St Albans, Hertfordshire
Phyllis Gregory (née Heffer), formerly of
  Warren House, Colney Heath
Dorothy Joan Gudgeon, St Albans, Hertfordshire
Gutteridge, Sleapshyde, Hertfordshire
Chris Hackett, Roe Green, Hatfield, Hertfordshire
Patricia Hall (née Gregory), Colney Heath,
  Hertfordshire
Mr and Mrs J.T. Halliwell, St Albans,
  Hertfordshire
Dr and Mrs R.P. Halliwell, Sandhurst, Berkshire
Avril Halsey, Colney Heath, Hertfordshire
Jacqueline Harrison, Sevenoaks, Roestock Lane
Rosemary Harrison (née Butland), Havant,
  Hampshire
Ms Cecilia Anne Hathaway, Colney Heath,
  Hertfordshire
Councillor John D.O. Henchley T.D (retired)
Gavin Horner, Park Corner, Colney Heath,
  Hertfordshire
Dennis and Jean Horner, Colney Heath,
  Hertfordshire
Alexander G. Howard, Colney Heath,
  Hertfordshire
Mr and Mrs D. Howard, Colney Heath,
  Hertfordshire
Roy Hudgell, Colney Heath, Hertfordshire
Hilary Hunt (née Butland), Rugby, Warwickshire
Derek Hylton, Colney Heath, Hertfordshire
Joyce Ilett, Bexley, Kent
Mr Ralph Clifford Jackson
Grace M. Jeffery, Colney Heath, Hertfordshire
Richard Kennan, Norwich/formerly of Nast Hyde
P.J. Kennedy, Colney Heath, Hertfordshire
Ken, Sylvia and Shirley Kentleton, Colney Heath,
  Hertfordshire
Beverley King, Colney Heath, Hertfordshire
Ronald P. and Olive M. Kingdon, North Mymms,
  Hertfordshire

Joan E. Knight, North Mymms, Hertfordshire
Clifford and Eileen Knowles, Coleby, Lincolnshire
Shirley and Brian Lambert, Welwyn Garden City
Mr Leigh Lambert, Gustard Wood
Amanda Lambert, Welwyn Garden City
Brenda M. Lawrence, Smallford, Hertfordshire
Ann Lee, Colney Heath, St Albans, Hertfordshire
Ted, Vilma and Richard Lewis, Colney Heath,
  Hertfordshire
Elizabeth Lewis (née Kennan),
  West Somerset/formerly of Nast Hyde
The Lewis Family, Franklin Close, Colney Heath,
  Hertfordshire
Alison K. Lilley, formerly of Moonrakers,
  Colney Heath, Hertfordshire
Richard and Gill Lilley, Markyate, Hertfordshire
Jenny and Alan Littlechild
Mr Bill Lloyd, formerly of Bullens, Green Lane,
  Colney Heath
Mr Russell Lloyd
Glen M. Lloyd, Colney Heath, Hertfordshire
Martin Lohan, Colney Heath, Hertfordshire
Robert and Celia Lord, Hitchin, Hertfordshire
Sonja and Andrew Lovett, Wheathampstead,
  Hertfordshire
Weston and Janet Marchant
The May Family
The Melvin Family, Colney Heath, Hertfordshire
Nicola Mitchell (née Hylton), Parkstreet,
  Hertfordshire
Joyce R. Moore and George R.
Dr R. Mortimer, Brisbane, Queensland, Australia
Keith and Joy Moyes, Grantham, Lincolnshire
Margaret Mary Murray, Smallford, Hertfordshire
Matthew J. Naylor, Sudbrooke, Lincolnshire
Dave and Sallie Notkins, Flitton, Bedfordshire
Miss C. O'Connor, Smallford, St Albans,
  Hertfordshire
Reginald J. Oakley, Colney Heath, Hertfordshire
Fred and Jean Olver, Hatfield, Hertfordshire
Henry and Margaret Parker and Family,
  Colney Heath, Hertfordshire
The Reverend John Patrick,
  Sleaford Parish Church
Leslie Payne, St Albans
Jake J. Penny, Colney Heath, Hertfordshire
D.J. Pile, Sleapshyde, St Albans, Hertfordshire
Mr W. (Gus) Pilley, Colney Heath, Hertfordshire
Sandy and Ed Pizzey, Hatfield, Hertfordshire

SUBSCRIBERS

Neil, Caroline, Fiona and Oliver Pluck,
Colney Heath, Hertfordshire

Robert W. Pointer, formerly of Colney Heath

Roger and Val Preston, London Colney,
Hertfordshire

Michael, Sue, James and Peter Rawlins,
Colney Heath, Hertfordshire

Adrian, Kate, Ian and Laura Reddish, Smallford,
Hertfordshire

Raymond A. Redwood, Colney Heath,
Hertfordshire

Maureen Renouf, Colney Heath, Hertfordshire

Brenda and Maurice Roberts, Colney Heath,
Hertfordshire

Brian Roberts, Colney Heath, Hertfordshire

Joshua Rodway, Tyttenhanger Green, St Albans

Dilys Rolls, Ashwater, Devon

Ren Rolls, St Albans

Mr John L. Rowland, Colney Heath, Hertfordshire

Andrew Sawyer, Colney Heath School

Paul D. Shinn, Colney Heath, Hertfordshire

Maureen A. Smith, Colney Heath Lane, St Albans,
Hertfordshire

Jane A. Smith, The Old Exchange, Colney Heath,
Hertfordshire

James and Stephanie Spanner, Colney Heath,
Hertfordshire

St Peter's Church, St Albans, Hertfordshire

Valaris E. Stapleton, Colney Heath, Hertfordshire

Monica K. Stoker, Colney Heath, Hertfordshire

Mitchell Taylor, Colney Heath, Hertfordshire

Ron Townshend, Stevenage, Hertfordshire

Mr Roy E. Turner, Colney Heath, Hertfordshire

Pauline Wallace, Vilamoura, Portugal

Margeret Webb, North Mymms, Hertfordshire

Mr Victor D. Webb, Colney Heath, Hertfordshire

Jim and Pam Whiting, The Cock, Colney Heath,
Hertfordshire

Phil Hamlyn Williams, Church House, Lincoln

David and Ann Willson, Hatfield, Hertfordshire

Mr and Mrs N.V. Wilmot, Sleapshyde

William and Joyce Winter, Smallford,
Hertfordshire

Fred and Sue Wonfor, Colney Heath,
Hertfordshire

Marie Wren, formerly of Tollgate Road

TITLES FROM THE SERIES

The Book of Addiscombe • Various
The Book of Addiscombe, Vol. II • Various
The Book of Bampton • Caroline Seward
The Book of Barnstaple • Avril Stone
Book of Bickington • Stuart Hands
Blandford Forum: A Millennium Portrait • Various
The Book of Bridestowe • R. Cann
The Book of Brixham • Frank Pearce
The Book of Buckland Monachorum & Yelverton • Hemery
The Book of Carshalton • Stella Wilks
The Parish Book of Cerne Abbas • Vale & Vale
The Book of Chagford • Ian Rice
The Book of Chittlehamholt with Warkleigh & Satterleigh • Richard Lethbridge
The Book of Chittlehampton • Various
The Book of Colney Heath • Bryan Lilley
The Book of Constantine • Moore & Trethowan
The Book of Cornwood & Lutton • Various
The Book of Creech St Michael • June Small
The Book of Cullompton • Various
The Book of Dawlish • Frank Pearce
The Book of Dulverton, Brushford, Bury & Exebridge • Various
The Book of Dunster • Hilary Binding
The Ellacombe Book • Sydney R. Langmead
The Book of Exmouth • W.H. Pascoe
The Book of Grampound with Creed • Bane & Oliver
The Book of Hayling Island & Langstone • Rogers
The Book of Helston • Jenkin with Carter
The Book of Hemyock • Clist & Dracott
The Book of Hethersett • Various
The Book of High Bickington • Avril Stone
The Book of Ilsington • Dick Wills
The Book of Lamerton • Ann Cole & Friends
Lanner, A Cornish Mining Parish • Scharron Schwartz & Roger Parker
The Book of Leigh & Bransford • Various
The Book of Litcham with Lexham & Mileham • Various
The Book of Loddiswell • Various
The Book of Lulworth • Rodney Legg
The Book of Lustleigh • Joe Crowdy
The Book of Manaton • Various
The Book of Markyate • Various
The Book of Mawnan • Various
The Book of Meavy • Pauline Hemery
The Book of Minehead with Alcombe • Binding & Stevens
The Book of Morchard Bishop • Jeff Kingaby
The Book of Newdigate • John Callcut
The Book of Northlew with Ashbury • Various
The Book of North Newton • Robins & Robins
The Book of North Tawton • Various
The Book of Okehampton • Radford & Radford
The Book of Paignton • Frank Pearce
The Book of Penge, Anerley & Crystal Palace • Various
The Book of Peter Tavy with Cudlipptown • Various
The Book of Pimperne • Jean Coull
The Book of Plymtree • Tony Eames
The Book of Porlock • Denis Corner
Postbridge – The Heart of Dartmoor • Reg Bellamy
The Book of Priddy • Various
The Book of Rattery • Various
The Book of Silverton • Various

The Book of South Molton • Various
The Book of South Stoke • Various
South Tawton & South Zeal with Sticklepath • Radfords
The Book of Sparkwell with Hemerdon & Lee Mill • Pam James
The Book of Staverton • Pete Lavis
The Book of Stithians • Various
The Book of Studland • Rodney Legg
The Book of Swanage • Rodney Legg
The Book of Torbay • Frank Pearce
Uncle Tom Cobley & All: Widecombe-in-the-Moor • Stephen Woods
The Book of Watchet • Compiled by David Banks
The Book of West Huntspill • Various
Widecombe-in-the-Moor • Stephen Woods
The Book of Williton • Michael Williams
Woodbury: The Twentieth Century Revisited • Roger Stokes
The Book of Woolmer Green • Various

FORTHCOMING

The Book of Bakewell • Various
The Book of Barnstaple, Vol. II • Avril Stone
The Book of Brampford • Various
The Book of Breage & Gurnoe • Stephen Polglase
The Book of the Bedwyns • Various
The Book of Bideford • Peter Christie
The Book of Bridport • Rodney Legg
The Book of Buckfastleigh • Sandra Coleman
The Book of Carharrack • Various
The Book of Castleton • Geoff Hill
The Book of Edale • Gordon Miller
The Book of Kingskerswell • Various
The Book of Lostwithiel • Barbara Frasier
The Book of Lydford • Barbara Weeks
The Book of Lyme Regis • Rodney Legg
The Book of Nether Stowey • Various
The Book of Nynehead • Various
The Book of Princetown • Dr Gardner-Thorpe
The Book of St Day • Various
The Book of Sampford Courtenay with Honeychurch • Stephanie Pouya
The Book of Sculthorpe • Garry Windeler
The Book of Sherborne • Rodney Legg
The Book of Southbourne • Rodney Legg
The Book of Tavistock • Gerry Woodcock
The Book of Thorley • Various
The Book of Tiverton • Mike Sampson
The Book of West Lavington • Various
The Book of Witheridge • Various
The Book of Withycombe • Chris Boyles

For details of any of the above titles or if you are interested in writing your own history, please contact: Commissioning Editor Community Histories, Halsgrove House, Lower Moor Way, Tiverton Business Park, Tiverton, Devon EX16 6SS, England; email: naomic@halsgrove.com

In order to include as many historic photographs as possible in this volume, a printed index is not included. However, the Community History Series is indexed by Genuki. For further information and indexes to volumes in the series, please visit: http://www.cs.ncl.uk/genuki/DEV/indexingproject.html